ULTIMATE GUIDE TO
DIRECT
SELLING

ULTIMATE GUIDE TO
DIRECT SELLING

Simple Tips to Increase Sales and Recruiting

karen phelps
direct selling success coach

Published by Advantage, Charleston, South Carolina.
Member of Advantage Media Group.

ADVANTAGE is a registered trademark and the Advantage colophon is a trademark of Advantage Media Group, Inc.

Printed in the United States of America.

ISBN: 978-1-59932-094-6
LCCN: 2008940762

Most Advantage Media Group titles are available at special quantity discounts for bulk purchases for sales promotions, premiums, fundraising, and educational use. Special versions or book excerpts can also be created to fit specific needs.

For more information, please write: Special Markets, Advantage Media Group, P.O. Box 272, Charleston, SC 29402 or call 1.866.775.1696.

Visit us online at **advantagefamily**.com

DEDICATION

This book is the culmination of countless hours of hard work and the loyal support of many people who encouraged my dreams of helping others find the success they are looking for from their direct selling business.

To these people I am forever grateful.

My husband Larry, for being behind this project every step of the way. His endless support keeps me constantly moving forward to provide systems and solutions for everyone in direct sales. To my sister Gette, and my son and daughter-in-law Bryan and Kristina who along with Larry keep things running smoothly at the office while I'm busy writing and editing. To my son Brandon and daughter-in-law Kirsten who have blessed me with Nickolas and Ryan. Being a grandparent is my favorite role in life and watching the boys helps me have fun and unwind! To my mother, the late Pat Essiambre, who sponsored me many years ago. She was a wonderful role model for how to mesh your business with your family. To my father, Louis Essiambre, who reads almost everything I write and listens to my recordings and always shares his thoughts with me. I'm glad you kept after me to get this book done! I'm forever grateful to my parents for my Catholic upbringing. I believe God has a plan for all of us and I'm so thankful I've been able to help others as He has intended. To my many siblings and other family members too numerous to mention, I love you all.

Thanks to the fantastic staff at Advantage Media, especially Amy Ropp. They are all so easy to work with and everyone does their best to make all of their authors look good!

To my graphic artist, Anthony Fisher, who has a knack of knowing what it takes to get the point across in a cartoon. I send you an idea and you work your magic. Thanks for all you do! To see his work go to www.fishfrytoon.com

To all my friends in direct selling, especially Cindy Juncaj who continually lets me bounce ideas off her and encouraged me to write this book. For the company executives who have allowed me to speak to their sales force, thank you for allowing me to make a difference in their lives.

To all of you who listen to learn, implement to grow, and share your successes with me daily, just knowing I helped make a difference keeps me working harder than ever to help you on your road to independence.

And finally, to all of you who read this book…I look forward to helping you love direct selling for what it is, "a wonderful way to help everyone reach their dreams."

CONTENTS

I was exposed to direct selling at an early age. My mother, Pat Essiambre, had worked with several direct selling companies over the years to help provide for our family of nine. When I was in high school I attended parties with my mom to model the fashions she was selling, and I helped the guests with their orders. No matter which company she was with, Mom was always one of the top sellers. She earned prizes and trips and the income was great.

I married Larry, my high school sweetheart, a year after we graduated from high school. Four years later our first son, Brandon, was born. I returned to work when he was a few months old. One beautiful August day when Brandon was two, I dropped him off at his daycare. When I walked to my car and turned to wave to him, there he stood in the picture window of the daycare, crying and reaching for me. I cried all the way to work.

That day was the day my life would change forever. I knew I couldn't work full time. I wanted to be home with my son. Bryan was born a few weeks before Brandon turned four. I left my job one week before my due date and I never worked for someone else again.

Now, the first year after Bryan was born was very challenging for us as a young family. We tried to tighten the budget and I worked cleaning houses and offices to help make ends meet. I never in my wildest dreams thought about joining a direct selling company. Larry and I had been discussing what I could do and he said, "Why don't you sell Queen's Way with your mother?" I don't know why not, maybe because I'm shy! But he encouraged me to call my mom, and the next day before I knew what happened I was a new consultant. Because Mom had done so many parties with family and my friends (I was a great hostess for her), I had very few people to help me get started in the business. My first year was not great. A few days before Larry's birthday I was anxiously awaiting a commission check that didn't arrive. I was frustrated and ready to quit. I was feeling pretty low when I borrowed money from my mom. I remember thinking, why is this happening to me? How could I make this business work so I could stay home with the boys?

Too stubborn to quit!

Well, you can probably guess, I didn't quit. I'm pretty stubborn and I didn't want to let my mom down. I started to do a few things differently at my parties and my schedule became pretty consistent. I even sponsored five people and was promoted to district leader on January 1, 1981. On January 2, three of my five recruits quit the business! Larry questioned whether I was good enough to be a leader, which was more than enough to irritate me and force me to prove him wrong! Two years later I was the number one district leader with our company and was promoted to regional advisor.

I began earning company trips and prizes my first full year with the company and my earnings were really helping us reach our goals. We took the boys to Disneyworld, put in an in-ground pool, and remodeled our modest home.

In February 1989 the wind was knocked out of my sails when the company I had grown so accustomed to closed its doors. I was devastated when my leader called me and asked me to come to a meeting to find out about another company we could join. I went and listened, and even though my heart wasn't in it, I decided to give it a try. They had given us the opportunity to join at the same level, but only two people from my previous team joined with me and they both quit soon after. A few months later I was questioning whether I was going to remain with the new company when someone approached me at a party about selling. Gina became my first recruit in the new company and she literally saved me—and my direct selling career. I had someone to work with again.

> *"Expect the best, plan for the worst, and prepare to be surprised." —Denis Waitley*

Sometimes it only takes one good thing to start the ball rolling again. I began booking more parties, sponsoring more people, and earned a trip my first year with the new company. I rebuilt my organization from the ground up, and was number one regional personal unit three years in a row. I learned from my mentors in the business and I was good at what I did. I also began to hold weekly trainings for my team, which lead to the promotion of fifteen directors and four regional directors from my personal team within one year. I loved direct selling and I loved my company.

When our company changed owners I stayed for a few years, but I knew it was time to move on. I had set a goal ten years prior to become an industry trainer, and it was the right time. I'd helped thousands while I was in the business and I knew I can help thousands more.

Through this book and the other training programs available on my website, I can show you how to work through the ups and downs of your business. Yes, we all have obstacles to overcome. They are there to make us stronger. If you're ready, I'll show you how you can accomplish more than you ever dreamed possible.

This book is for you if you are either looking to join a direct selling company or you are part of one already.

You will notice I have kept the language of the book simple. This is not a difficult business and I do not intend to complicate it for you. My intent is to show you how to develop simple systems to produce fantastic results.

Through the years it became apparent to me that when I asked more questions I had better results. I will be asking many questions throughout this book to help you discover the areas you need to develop in your business.

I'll provide you with scripts that were effective for me. I realize everyone is different. We all have different personalities and comfort levels. Feel free to take a script and tweak it to fit you and your personality.

*Why do people
join a direct
selling company?*

Read on...

CHAPTER ONE

Why So Many People Are Flocking to this Lifestyle Friendly Business

Direct selling is an opportunity for everyone to live the American dream of owning their own business. I know because I lived the dream for over twenty years!

There are many obstacles people must overcome as business owners. One of the major hurdles is financial investment. It takes an overwhelming amount of money to open a franchise. Beginning a direct selling business is like opening a franchise in your home. The start-up costs are minimal, and you can begin earning a substantial income immediately. The second thing that prevents people from having their own business is lack of time. If you are working a full-time job and you want to start your own business, you probably don't have the necessary time it will take to pursue this new opportunity. Direct selling is the answer for people who are looking for freedom to work their business when they want and the ability to earn a substantial income.

Direct selling is the business of selling person-to-person. You can do this through one-on-one sales, home parties, or network marketing. What distinguishes direct selling from the other types of selling is that it's a "people business." Direct selling professionals solve people's problems by providing them with products, services, and business opportunities. There are many reasons people begin a direct selling business, but the two that stand out are the opportunity to earn an above average income and the flexibility of working the business around personal and family obligations.

According to statistics provided by the Direct Selling Association, in 2006 89.9 percent of people work part-time; this is less than thirty hours a week. The major advantage to having a direct selling business is that you can often produce more income than you could at a full-time job. Most people join to supplement rather than replace their income. Once they begin to realize success, they begin thinking, "If I work my business a little bit harder and invest a few extra hours into it, I can actually make a lot more." According to the 2006 DSA statistics, the retail sales of the direct selling companies in the United States were over thirty-two billion dollars, and there were 15.2 million direct sellers at that time in the United States.

The state of the economy indicates there are a large percentage of families living above their means. They don't have quite as much money at the end of the week or the end of the month as they need. Even though their earnings are consistent, the "spendable income" is reduced by inflation. Families are looking for a way to supplement their earnings. This is an easy way for a stay-at-home mom, working mother, single person, retiree, or husband and wife team to increase the monthly "spendable income" that comes into their household.

Direct Sales Is Booming!

Many investors including Warren Buffett are seeing the value of owning all or a piece of successful direct selling companies. Major corporations whose products have withstood the elements of time have established a direct selling channel as another means of getting their products and services out to more people. Now is the perfect time to view this industry for what it is. It really does offer an incredible opportunity to supplement earnings and improve your lifestyle!

We want it all, and for a lot of us what we're doing is not going to produce the income that will provide us with everything we want. A "little extra money" is the number one reason people join a direct selling company. It is not the main reason why people stay in direct selling, but it is a major motive as to why they join. My philosophy is, "You can make as little as you want in direct selling or as much as you want in direct selling, and the choice is totally up to you!" The average person who joins would be satisfied with an extra two hundred dollars per week. Just think about what an extra eight hundred to one thousand dollars per month would make in your family's household income.

What keeps people in the business is the realization many of their peers are earning substantially more than one thousand dollars per month. They become aware of leaders within their own company who are earning fifty thousand, one hundred thousand, or even $250,000 per year and more. Once a person becomes aware of the real opportunity that awaits them, the only question left to answer is "Am I willing to turn this part-time income into a full-time income opportunity?" Ask yourself, "Are you willing to do what it takes, without making any excuses, to earn what others are earning?" Thousands of people in direct selling are earning six-figure incomes, and all of them have made the choice to "work their business." It really is not a difficult choice to make!

People Want Flexibility

Even though the number one reason people join is for the money, over the years I have sponsored many people who wanted something else. Some were not quite fulfilled as stay-at-home moms, and some joined to be able to purchase products for a discount. Others joined because they loved the products and wanted to share the products with friends and family, and the earnings were just a bonus. The majority of people in direct selling who are stay-at-home moms choose to be home with their children, so a flexible schedule is probably their reason for joining. You set your work schedule! You can work this business around your family. You can set your hours around whatever your family schedule is, and it becomes a very lifestyle friendly business. You also have the opportunity to include your family in some of activities you are doing with your direct selling business.

As I mentioned previously, many people are looking for a way to make ends meet. But a large number of working moms are also looking for a way to replace an income they gave up when they chose to stay home with the children. There are more two-income families than ever before in history, but it is often by necessity not choice. These families may need the income from two paychecks to make ends meet, but it doesn't necessarily mean Mom wants to work outside the home. Some families decide it is better to put off frivolous purchases to allow Mom to stay home during the early childhood years. She is invited to a "home party" and observes the consultant, who is also a mother of two small children and having fun and making money at the same time! Mom begins to imagine, "If I did this a few evenings each week,

I would still be able to be home with the kids but I could have a little extra money each month for some of the extras we've been putting off." All of a sudden a light bulb goes off and she thinks, "Wow. Maybe this could be the answer for me, too."

It's a Great Opportunity for Everyone

Again, according to the DSA statistics of 2006, 85 percent of direct sellers are female. Direct selling has changed and evolved over the years. Even though the most recent statistics show the median age of consultants is forty-four, there is more age diversity in the industry than at any other time. The direct selling industry is an attractive opportunity for young singles that join to earn extra income to support their single income household or to pay off student loans. Single moms often have a direct selling business because it's convenient to schedule their business activities around their full-time job and parenting. More and more people who have retired from their full-time jobs look for a way to supplement their retirement earnings. People are living longer and have more active lifestyles than in the past. Beginning a direct selling business when they retire can easily help provide them with the means to enjoy life after retirement without continually tapping into their savings! In fact when I was actively working my direct selling business, one of the top people in my team was Donna, who did not start selling until she was in her sixties. Her husband had retired, and she always told me, "I started selling because I realized we were seeing a little bit too much of each other." She loved working her direct selling business, and her number one reason for doing so was to purchase gifts for her children and grandchildren for their birthdays and for Christmas. Once her husband retired, it was necessary to supplement their retirement income.

Most of the companies have low startup fees. Some offer a kit used to demonstrate the products. Each company has its own kit policies. The kit options range from purchasing a kit with an option to earn back all or part of your investment in cash, to free products by selling a predetermined amount within a specific timeframe, to receiving a free kit which again you must qualify for within a specific timeframe. Some companies allow you to invest in inventory which when sold provides you with instant profits. In order to maintain a growing business, the consultant must be diligent with reordering products so the inventory does not become depleted.

When you compare the cost of starting a franchise, which can range from seventy-five thousand to one million dollars or more to beginning a direct selling business for one thousand dollars or less, it's easy to see why more and more people are attracted to direct selling. They are provided with a means to begin their own business without having the worry of building a company from the ground up.

Your Business Is Ready to Go When You Are!

Another bonus of joining a direct selling company is that you don't have to worry about anything because it is all done for you. Established companies have training and systems in place to help your business run smoothly and effectively. Most companies provide great training manuals to guide you at every level of your business and teach you step by step how to succeed. How do I work my business? How do I go from Point A to Point B? How do I get my first bookings? How I make my first phone calls? How do I get my business launched so I immediately begin earning money? It is much easier to have a great start when you don't have to figure everything out on your own.

An additional advantage direct sellers have is the support of their upline leaders. In addition to the person who sponsored you there are often many levels of leaders who are available for support, training, and encouragement. You may have many upline leaders who will be actively working with you to help you succeed. The important thing to remember is to embrace the training and support offered, as you will move towards success faster this way than by trying to do everything on your own. Companies are aware that direct selling is a "people helping people" business and they are sure to have a home office staff willing to go the extra mile to answer your questions and solve any problems that may arise. It's wonderful knowing that once you launch your new business there are many people who are willing and able to support and guide you every step of the way. This is much different than starting your own business from the ground floor and having no one to learn from. In direct selling, it's not hard to find a person, manual, or training guide with answers to your questions.

People join a company because they are influenced by the products. They may critique several business opportunities, but ultimately a person must feel good about representing a company and the products they provide in order to succeed. I've never known a successful salesperson who didn't like the products he or she was selling. Yes, you will be selling products, so factor this in when deciding which company to join. The good news is that you will not have to search out suppliers for products. Your company is going to be supplying the products, which will allow you more time to sell and earn. All you need to do is demonstrate and show the value of your products, explain what makes your products different and better, close the sale, and put your earnings in the bank.

What do you need to

do to get started?

Read on...

CHAPTER TWO

How to Jump-start Your Business
for Instant Rewards

New consultants who set earnings goals will earn more and will begin earning sooner than those who do not take time to set an earnings goal when they join. If you have been in the business for a while, it's not too late to set an earnings goal. Once you do you will notice an improvement in your business as you continually work to reach your goal.

There are three parts to goal setting. First, decide how much money you want to earn. Second, you need to know what you want to do with the money you earn from your direct selling business. Then you need to know how soon you want to begin earning to move you closer to your goal.

What Do You Want from Your Business?

When consultants have goals in place they,

- are more focused because they know what they are working for.
- create a plan of action to help them reach their goal.
- begin working their business immediately.

They don't join and then wait for weeks or months to begin their business. They are anxious to start working immediately.

Just because you want money doesn't necessarily mean you will work to get it. Everyone wants or needs more money. Set a precise goal: "I want two thousand dollars to pay off my Visa" and you will begin to look for ways to accomplish the goal. It is vital for you to know what you want to do with your earnings. Once you discover your main goal and objective, whether it is saving for a family vacation, paying down credit card debt, or saving for retirement, you will begin to focus on what you need to do to reach your goal. It will provide you with a reason to work your business other than just working to "make more money."

Say Carol joins my company and decides she wants six hundred dollars for a new dishwasher, and that she wants to purchase it within the next two months. Carol needs to have three hundred dollars a month for the next two months in order to purchase the dishwasher. She knows what she wants and she becomes focused on achieving her goal.

The timeframe for your earnings goals will vary. It will depend on what you are currently working for. You may have a thirty-day goal to earn five to six hundred dollars for a weekend getaway for your anniversary, or you may be working on a yearlong goal of taking your family on a vacation to Disneyworld® that will cost around four thousand dollars. If you are still new to direct selling, begin with a goal you can accomplish within three to six months. New consultants who set and reach a goal within their first three to six months will have a decent start in their business and will stay in the business longer.

You need to know how much time you can devote to your business or you will find yourself not putting in any time at all. If you haven't decided how many hours per week you can work in your direct selling business, DO IT NOW! There is nothing worse than having a business and not showing up for work. You need to ask yourself, "How many hours can I devote to my direct selling business?" You also need to know when you are going to work. Set a schedule to work your business around your family and other activities, which is one of the biggest draws to direct selling. Once you know how many hours per week you can work and you schedule your work around your family, you will realize how easy it is to have a home-based direct selling business.

If you are not sure how much time to schedule for each activity ask your sponsor or leader to help you with your schedule. They can help determine how much time is needed for each activity. They will let you know how much time the average consultant needs before, during, and after each party. You will reap from your business what you sow in the beginning. You must first invest your time before you see results.

It's Time to Go to Work

The great thing about being in direct selling is you have your own business with flexibility. You can always adjust your schedule as you need to. Be careful that you do not become too complacent in your business. You don't want to use excuses for not working your business, and if you have to adjust your time, you need to realize you will also have to adjust your earnings. You can't expect to spend less time working the business and still make the same amount. You may need to adjust the amount of time you can work the business because of a family illness or something that comes up that needs more of your time. Isn't it wonderful to know it's okay if you need time off? It's easy to adjust your time, and having your own direct selling business allows you the flexibility to do so. Just be prepared to readjust and reevaluate your goals so you do not become frustrated and discontent with your business.

Of course, your time is going to be spent more effectively if you are trained properly and are following the correct paths. Consultants who take time to be trained in the business will increase their success ratio. Let's pretend instead of joining a direct selling company you take a teller position at a local bank. Could you begin your job and not have any training? Of course not! You can't show up the first day of work and say, "I'm very good at math and numbers, so I don't need any training. I know how to work an adding machine." Even if you have been a teller at another bank, you need to know what your responsibilities are and you will have to learn new systems. Joining a direct selling company is no different than starting any other job. You need to ask, "What do I need to know and what do I have to do in order to increase my chances of success?" Taking time to learn the business is one of the first steps on your path to success.

Be the Best You Can Be

Most people don't join a direct selling company and say, "I want to be mediocre." Anyone who does not make time for training and take advantage of the training provided is on their way to having a mediocre business that will rarely provide the results they are looking for.

The best training is to observe another consultant's party. It is just like job shadowing. You need to know what to do at every party that will achieve the results you are looking for. When you watch your sponsor or leader you learn not only what to do but why you need to do it. It helps you learn the techniques you need to implement when you begin working your own business.

If you are a sponsor or leader, encourage your new consultants to observe you at a couple of parties. They will often observe something on the second party, which they did not notice during the first. Always allow time for follow up questions.

Don't be afraid to shadow or to observe your leaders. Some leaders have been in the business for a long time and a lot of them are very, very good. Don't compare yourself to them, or watch them and think, "Oh, my gosh. I'm never going to be able to do my business exactly like this person." Instead, ask yourself, "How can I make what she is doing fit me and my personality so that I get the same results?"

Shadowing is very important, but in the end, your go-to training tool will always be the company's training manual. I have worked with so many companies over the last several years, and the training manuals are absolutely phenomenal. What bothers and shocks me the most is how few people have actually read their company training manual. Now I know that on the job training is the best, but don't you want to know everything you can about your company, product, and the opportunity? I've done training for consultants who have been in the business for at least a year and who have never opened their training manuals. If you want to succeed in this business and your company has provided you with an online or physical training manual, take time to read it! You will be surprised to find the answers to many of your questions in your company training manual. Read it, reread it, highlight it, and use it as a resource guide. This is your company's sales bible for how to succeed in the business.

Let Everyone Know You Are Open for Business

Now that you have set your earnings goal, delegated time for your business, and participated in recommended training, the next step is to have an open-for-business party. This party will launch your new business. Or if you've been in business for a while and your business has stalled, you may want to re-launch. Imagine opening your business in a storefront on Main Street. What would you do to get customers? You would have a grand opening. You would invite people to come and check out your new store. You would let people know your store is now open for business.

Even though you don't have a storefront you still must let everyone know you are open for business. So your open-for-business party, your grand opening, your business launch, whatever your company calls it, it's your party to get the word out. The party should be scheduled within your first seven to ten days of joining your direct selling company. You need to let everyone know you have started a new direct selling business. You are really excited and you want to demonstrate the products you are going to be representing with your new direct selling business.

There are several things a consultant can do to maximize the results of her open-for-business party. The first thing that must be done is to create a list. Begin writing down names of everyone you know. Don't prejudge people and don't ask if they want to come before you mail your invitations. Send invitations to everyone you know. It will be easier to create your list if you begin to put guests into groups. Invite friends, family, acquaintances, neighbors, co-workers, and people you know through your kids. Keep writing. You'll be surprised by how many people you know. Most people can easily list between fifty and one hundred names to invite. Again, don't prejudge anyone. Send everyone an invitation. You will have better results when you mail an invitation to everyone.

"The Fortune is in the Follow Up" —Unknown

The most important thing is to make follow-up calls to everyone. You cannot just mail invitations and not follow up. These calls are important, as you can let everyone know you are a new consultant and this is your open-for-business party. You want to begin earning as soon as possible.

When I was actively sponsoring people in the business I would ask them, "How soon do you want to start earning?" Most would say, "Well, I want to start earning money right away." I would then reply, "Okay, you need to schedule your open-for-business party as soon as possible within the next seven to fourteen days." I created a sense of urgency for them to hold this party as well as her initial bookings right away. It's very easy for new consultants to book parties when they join because they are enthusiastic. They think, "I've made a great decision." They call their friends and share their enthusiasm and excitement.

New consultants begin booking their first parties on sheer enthusiasm. It's easy to say to your friends, "I'm really excited. I joined this direct selling company and I need a few friends to book parties to help me get started in my business." Most new consultants are not aware of their company hostess program and the benefits the hostess will enjoy. The enthusiasm for their new business enables them to ask without fear of rejection and their business is off to a great start.

Break It Down

Once you have your list you will need to break it down even more. List those people with whom you would feel the most comfortable doing your first parties. This is a new venture for you. It's different from what you've done in the past, and you will probably be slightly nervous while you are doing your first few parties. So hold these parties for the friends or family members you will feel the most comfortable with.

New consultants need to book from as many areas of their lives as possible. Don't book all family members or all neighbors. Doing so will quickly lead to a dead-end business. Book a few family members, a few neighbors, a co-worker, and friend from the gym. Book a few people you've met at your child's school or at sporting events, and one or two members of your church. Look at different areas of your life, get one or two bookings from each different area, and you will soon have a growing, thriving business.

It's easy to identify people to help you get started in the business when you review the list you created for your open-for-business party.

How many parties you do each week depends on your goals. Do you want to hold two per week? Three or more? How much do you want to earn? Do you want to have two hundred dollars in weekly earnings, or more? Go back to the number you decided before, and make sure you know what your company average party and average earnings per party are, as this will help you set your weekly income goal. If your company average earnings per party are one hundred dollars then you will meet your weekly earnings goal of two hundred with only two parties.

A new consultant who wants to hold two parties per week should book at least eight parties in her first thirty days, which is two parties a week for her first four weeks in the business. A full booking calendar is however many parties a consultant wants to do per week for four weeks out in the business. Teaching new consultants to do this immediately helps develop consistency in the business.

Get off to a Fast Start

Most companies will have a Quick Start or Fast Start program which recognizes new consultants with incentives for achieving specified sales and or sponsoring level within their first thirty, sixty or ninety days. New consultants will definitely want to set a goal to reach the company quick-start or fast-start levels. These are usually great incentives or additional items for their kits and most are easily earned by holding one or two parties each week. If you are a new consultant make sure you know what you need to do to earn your company's quick-start or fast-start programs, but keep your main focus on your earnings goal and you will most likely earn all of the new consultant prizes.

Leader Tip: If you are a leader make sure your new consultant remains focused on her earnings goal; if her earnings goal is less than she needs to reach her quick-start make sure she is aware of the requirements and the prizes, as she will most likely want to do an extra party or two to earn her prize.

Leader Tip: If you are a sponsor be careful of your word choices. You should ask, "How much do you want to earn per week?" instead of "How much would you like to earn per week?" which sets them up to earn less.

Leader Tip: Always discuss weekly income versus monthly income. This will encourage a new consultant to visualize the business as a consistent source of income rather than a hobby.

Are you wondering whether or not you have what it takes to succeed in direct selling?

Read on....

CHAPTER THREE

How to Create the Mindset and Habits
of a Successful Entrepreneur

The one thing you will discover in this business is if you're not optimistic, you're not going to succeed. You'll encounter people who will be negative about your business. When I first joined, people would say to me, "You're going to do what? Can't you get a real job?" You must have a positive attitude to respond to them confidently, "Yes, and I'm so excited."

If you can develop and maintain a positive mental attitude, you will become more confident in yourself and your business. You will feel confident that you've made the right decision to begin your direct selling business. This helps you to work through any ups and downs you may have. I never realized the importance of being self-motivated until I became involved with direct selling. I was a motivated person and self-starter, but I never realized it or thought about it much until I began my sales career. I soon realized if I didn't go to work, I wasn't going to get paid. I believe it was sheer luck that my first year in the business I attended a Zig Ziglar seminar with my leader and several other consultants. I was so motivated and pumped that day. I bought both of Zig's audio programs, *How to Stay Motivated* and *Secrets of Closing the Sale*. I listened to those training tapes over and over again for years. For probably twenty years, they were my favorite training and motivation tapes.

Make Time for Listening to Motivational Materials

People often ask me, "When is the best time to listen to motivational CDs? Do you listen to them when you're down? Do you listen to them when you're up?" I reply, "You have to listen or read motivational or inspirational material every day." Thirty years ago I decide to get up early each morning so I could make sure to get my daily dose of exercise and motivation. I still walk, ride my bicycle, or use a weight machine three to five times per week for forty-five minutes to an hour. During my entire exercise time I listen to motivational or training materials. This has always been very helpful for me, and I recommend it for everyone. It has really helped me focus on the positive aspects of my life and business.

"Unless you change how you are, you will always have what you've got." —Jim Rohn

Many people find it difficult to stay motivated without having a boss breathing down their neck. I remind them that the great news about being in a direct selling business is that you're the boss. You don't have to answer to anyone. The bad news is that you're also the employee, and sometimes the employee is not as good as the boss would like them to be. So you have to ask yourself, "What kind of employee do I want to have working for me?" Your answer should be someone who is a goal oriented with a positive attitude, and disciplined to work the business when the boss is not around!

Discipline Yourself to Work Your Business Consistently

A lot of direct sellers are not focused and in control of their business. Lack of discipline usually leads to disappointment in themselves and the business. You need to be disciplined enough to work your business in spite of any obstacles. When you are consistent you will notice you don't face a lot of the same challenges as others in the business. The economy rarely affects your sales or sponsoring, and you have less aggravated customers than those who are not focused and fail to follow up.

Less disciplined people tend to take things a little bit too personally, and often put their business on the side burner when a positive attitude combined with disciplined actions would move them through an obstacle or challenge. You need to ask yourself, "What are the actions I need to take that will produce the income I want in my direct selling business?" I call these *income-producing activities*. They include making phone calls, holding parties, and scheduling interviews to bring people into the business. You must also attend trainings and meetings if you are a consultant and hold trainings and meetings if you are a leader.

You need to include time for all of these tasks in your schedule. If you have decided to work your business full-time and this is your only source of earnings, you must make sure you are doing exactly what you would expect your employees to do if you were an employer.

Sometimes we have spouses, family members, or friends that are not supportive of our business; we tend to react to what they're saying. As I mentioned previously, nine months after I began my direct selling business I became a director. I had sponsored five people to become a director and was promoted to the position on January 1, 1981. On January 3, three of my five people quit. My husband said to me, "I guess you're not good enough to be a leader." (He assures me he was joking and just wanted to push my buttons.) Well, for me, those were fighting words and I decided to prove him wrong. The following year I was in the top twenty for sponsoring.

When you think about it; our spouses, family, and friends want to protect us. They think we may have gotten "sucked into something" or that we joined without really thinking it through. These people tend to become nervous and overprotective. Often it's hard to ignore them, but that's what you have to do. You have to ignore what they're saying and reaffirm to yourself why you're in the business and what you want out of it. If they're saying, "You're not going to succeed," my gut instinct would be this response: "Well, you know what? You think I'm not going to succeed in this business, but I'll show you. I'm going to work hard and I'm going to prove you wrong. I'm going to show you that I *am* capable of doing this business and becoming successful at it."

Even though you may want to eliminate all the negative people from your life it's not always easy to do so, but you can decide to not focus on what they're saying. You can choose to react to what is being said around you and about you, or you can ignore it and go on your merry way! That's why it's so important to have a positive attitude.

When you have a positive attitude, you can handle the negatives that will come into your life. You'll be able to ignore the people who tell you to get a real job. Wow, I guess you can tell I was exposed to some negative feelings over the years!

"Optimism creates energy and is contagious." —Denis Waitley

Avoid the Quicksand Crowd

Staying positive has not been a challenge for me over the years, until recently. My husband Larry is retired and he loves to turn on the news first thing in the morning! I've never been one to watch television in the morning. I just don't turn it on. Remember, I get up and listen to motivational tapes while I exercise, and I might turn some classical music on when I'm working my business. I'll have background noise, but I never got used to having the news or talk shows on in the morning. When he retired and I started listening to the news while I made breakfast in the kitchen I began to think, "This is so depressing. How can I have a productive day when I begin it listening to all this negativity?"

Some people wake up to the news and go to bed to the news and then wonder why they have such a negative outlook on life! How do you expect to have good dreams if you fall asleep after watching all the violence shown on the daily news? That's not saying I don't listen a little or scan the headlines of the paper. But I can't remain focused and keep myself positive if I'm only listening to what the media tells me, which is 99 percent negative. If you took a newspaper and put red Xs on every single article in the paper that was negative you would probably find 90 to 95 percent of the news is not worth reading.

So try not to read the newspaper except for some quick headlines, watch a minimum amount of television, and don't begin or end your day watching the news. Begin your day listening to motivational, inspirational, or training tapes and you'll notice a positive change in your disposition and your attitude.

I often use Eeyore and Winnie the Pooh as my examples. Winnie the Pooh has a wonderful day all the time and Eeyore is always moping and expecting the worst to happen. Only you can choose how you will begin your day. Will you start it with motivation and inspiration from the many CDs in your personal development library, or will you begin your day with the gloom and doom of the daily news?

Take Time to Be Thankful

"The happiest people in the world are those who have a hard time recalling their worries and an easy time remembering their blessings." —Alin Austin

If you don't already have one it's time to make a gratitude list. Having a gratitude list helps to maintain focus on all your blessings and all the positive aspects of your business and personal life. You should be grateful for your family, your spouse, your children, your sponsor in the business, your leaders in the business, your company that provides you with great opportunity, and the fantastic products. Being thankful helps you maintain a more positive attitude.

Direct selling is the business of people helping people, and as a new consultant; you should expect to receive some training from your sponsor and your leaders. You may have been sponsored by someone who is also fairly new in the business and who doesn't know the business well enough to provide you with proper training. Most likely this person's leader will be responsible for your training and will offer the support and encouragement you need.

It's great to know you have a support team of people who want you to succeed. The more contact you have with your leaders and the more you use the training tools and study the systems your company has in place, the greater your chances for success. Learn to take advice from your leaders, as they want to help you succeed in your direct selling business.

New consultants have a right to know what type of support they will receive when they join. You may want to ask, "What type of training will I have? What are you going to do for me to help me succeed?" Sometimes you have to take the bull by the horns. You have to say, "I want to succeed in this business." If at your interview you express your desire to earn one thousand dollars each month, make sure you know what actions you need to take to make your goal a reality. Good leaders love assertive new recruits who take charge of their business immediately. An assertive new consultant will ask, "How am I going to learn that? What type of training will I receive? Can I come and watch you do home parties?" This kind of consultant wants and expects to learn everything she can to succeed in the business.

Performance Is the Direct
Result of Expectation

"All of us perform better and more willingly when we know why we're doing what we have been told or asked to do." —Zig Ziglar

People often sponsor someone into the company and then back off for fear of creating too much pressure. They think, "I don't want to push this new recruit too much because if I do, she'll resist or quit." Don't be afraid to set your expectations high for yourself as well as others you sponsor into the business. If you are the type of person who wants to succeed and you feel you are not getting the help you need, ask for your leader's assistance. Make sure you don't whine or complain. You could say, "I feel like I need a little bit more training and support. Can I attend another party to observe you? What can I do in order to get the training that I need? What events can I attend? Are there meetings where this will be covered?"

When you choose to ask questions rather than make statements your sponsor or leader will not feel as though she is being challenged. If you approach your leader with an open mind and say, "You know what? I really want to learn as much as I can. I really want to succeed in this business. I see myself making six-figure-a-year income. What can I do? Where can I learn? What are the resources we have to help me become more successful?" I guarantee you she will take you under her wing and teach you everything you need to know. She'll be thinking, "Wow, I have a dynamo here. She definitely wants to succeed in this business and I'm anxious to help her all I can."

I remember when my first company went out of business and I joined the second. I met a very powerful woman who was the number one leader of the company. I observed Marlene for a few months, and I watched her outgoingness and her willingness to share with people. She had given me her phone number at a previous meeting, but I had resisted calling her. I kept thinking, "Oh, she's not going to want to talk to me because I'm not on her team. She's not making money on me."

One day I finally got up the nerve to call her. I said, "Hey, Marlene, this is Karen. You know what? I've been watching you for a few months. You are such a dynamite leader. I want to be where you are. I want to make the kind of money you're making. I want the big monthly paychecks just like you're getting. What do you do? How can I do what you do?"

She was so surprised that I had actually taken the time to call her. She said, "Karen, over the years you are the only one outside of my team who has actually asked me how I built my business." I was shocked. She then willingly spent an hour and a half on the phone explaining to me her secrets to success, and we became very good friends after that. Imagine that. Even though I was her competition she was still willing to share her secrets. That's what is so amazing about this business. It truly is a business of "people helping people." Find the person you want to emulate and ask for her best success strategy. She will most likely be flattered and willing to help you find success.

Is This an Obstacle or a Stepping-stone?

"Keep your face to the sunshine and you cannot see the shadow." —Helen Keller

When you encounter negativity or someone who might not want to help out, you always have a choice. You may experience some business challenges, and it will not help your business if you quit after each little circumstance that doesn't go the way you want it to. Every job opportunity brings its challenges. Whether you have a direct selling business or are working in the corporate world, you'll have ups and downs. The survivors in life work through obstacles and challenges and view them as opportunities to grow.

Someone who has had a bad start in the business, who has signed on but hasn't really begun to work the business, can still be very successful. In fact, some of my most successful consultants were those who did very little in the business their first thirty to sixty days but stuck with it and went on to have outstanding success. A new consultant could have a few parties to begin but not enough to reach her desired earnings goal.

You must continually ask yourself, "Am I doing what it takes in order to earn the income I desire?" If not, it's time to get going! Learn from your failures, and don't be afraid to start all over again. Take some time to evaluate what didn't work and do it differently next time. You have training and support available, so take advantage of it and then start again. You need to, "pick yourself up, brush yourself off, and start all over again!"

Most successful people who have long careers in direct selling would not be where they are today had they quit at the first sight of adversity. "Winners never quit, and quitters never win."

A key component to your success is to discover your activity-to-results ratio. For example, say you are making your follow-up phone calls and in one evening make four calls. From those four phone calls you secure one party, which eventually produces six hundred dollars in sales, of which you receive a one-hundred-fifty-dollar commission. You repeat the pattern the next two weeks and have the same results each time.

It's time to figure out your ratio. Twelve phone calls produced three bookings. Each booking produced six hundred dollars in sales, of which you earned one hundred fifty dollars in commissions. Therefore, for every four phone calls you make you can expect to earn one hundred fifty dollars in commission. Once you have figured out your ratio, you need to condition yourself to do the activities that will produce the results you need!

It's a simple equation:
ACTIVITY = RESULTS = EARNINGS!

The less consistent you are the more up and down cycles you are likely to experience. Become consistent and have an evenly balanced calendar. Use your activity-to-results ratio to help plan what needs to be done to avoid dips in your business. If you just move along in the business, believing there will be easy times and hard times no matter what you do, you will find yourself in periodic dry spells. Go back to doing what it takes to maintain or achieve your earnings goals. Many direct sellers create ups and downs in the business because they expect it to happen. You may have overheard someone say, "Don't worry; it's just part of the business." Sometimes leaders who mean well inadvertently plant things in our minds without even realizing it. A leader will say, "If you want to hold two parties per week then book three parties because one of them is going to cancel." And the programming begins. Now you expect one of three bookings to cancel, which is not necessarily the case if you perfect your hostess coaching—but that's another chapter.

"Remember there is plenty of room at the top-but not enough to sit down." —Zig Ziglar

You must develop good habits for your business.

- You must get out and meet people. You must network. Times are changing along with technology. People are home sitting in front of their computers. You will not meet people when you're sitting at your computer. You have to get out of your house. You have to socialize, network, and ask for referrals.
- You must learn to love your phone. In direct selling a "silent phone" means a "dead business." If you are not calling you are not earning.
- The number one habit you must cultivate to become successful in direct selling is setting a weekly schedule for your business. Don't view your business only in terms of what you must do each month. Make a list of weekly activities and plan your weekly schedule. This will help you create the success you desire from your business. An important reminder: work on your business when you have scheduled time for it. You may have scheduled in two parties for the week but only

booked one. Use the second time slot to make more phone calls. You only need six ten-minute time slots to make calls for one hour each week. Setting aside sixty minutes for phone calls each week is much easier than setting aside four hours during the month. When you create a schedule for yourself, *you will get more done!* Schedule time to work your business the same way you schedule all your other activities. If you have planned to pick up your kids at three o'clock from school, you will be there to pick up them up at three o'clock. Work your business the same way. If you're planning to do a party every Monday and Wednesday night, you will do everything you can to make sure you have a party scheduled for Monday night and Wednesday night each week.

- Attend all of your local meetings. Your attendance at meetings is important for your success. The motivation you will get just from being around your peers is one of the best things you can do for yourself. You want to receive all the education you can. At each monthly meeting you will learn new strategies and new techniques that will help you take your business to the next level. You want to receive any and all recognition you've earned. Your local leaders will recognize the top sellers and top sponsors on her team. Observing others receiving recognitions inspires you to want to do more.

- Attend company sponsored meetings and conventions. You will be motivated, educated, and inspired to become the best you can be. I had only been in direct selling for seven months when I attended my first convention. The sight of everyone walking across the stage and receiving their awards and flowers was amazing. I sat in the audience thinking to myself, "I want to walk across the stage next year." And I did! The recognition at company conventions is unbelievable. If you don't walk across the stage the first time you attend, you will set your goal to be on stage next year. Attending your company's convention can really turn you on in the business. Even if you think to yourself, "I can't afford it," go, because once you see the success of others in the business, your hope will be renewed and you will be inspired. You'll likely think, "If they can do it, so can I!"

You want to keep motivated. You want to stay educated and updated. You definitely want the recognition you deserve. Anything is possible when you believe!

Leader Tip: Have a lending library of motivational and training materials to lend out to active members of your team.

Leader Tip: Have team members create a gratitude list during a meeting. Remind them to post it somewhere they will see it often.

What do you need to do

to get bookings?

Read on....

CHAPTER FOUR

Discover the Secrets to Becoming
a "Fantastic Booker"

It has always been a mystery to me why people would not want to hold home parties. Where else can you party for a living, make a phenomenal amount of money, and receive *free food* every time you go out?

The more I think about it the more I realize it's because they have a fear of rejection. No one likes to hear the word *no*. Consultants may also dislike asking someone to do a favor for them. When you hold an open-for-business party and when you book your initial parties, you are asking someone to help you get started in your business.

A consultant may not want to hold parties because she isn't sure what to do. Not everyone who is in direct selling holds home parties. A new consultant could have been sponsored by somebody who sets individual appointments to sell rather than selling to a group at a home party. A consultant could have had a bad experience at a home party. Perhaps she was a guest at a home party with an obnoxious consultant. Because of her bad experience she develops a stereotype and believes everyone who does home parties is pushy and obnoxious, and there's no way she will follow suit.

Those are all reasons why you might not want to hold home parties. So why *should* you hold home parties? Because you can spend the same amount of time showing your products to one person as you will to eight, ten, and twelve people at a time. Which commissions check do you want the one from the sales of eight to ten customers or the one from one customer? A home party for eight to ten people will take approximately two and a half hours, while selling to one individual at a time may require one and a half hours. A little more time nets a much larger commission check.

Holding Home Parties Will Multiply Your Results

You will also be exposed to more people at one time. Your business will grow faster when you do home parties and group presentations. You are the salesperson and you will do the demonstration for the party. You will earn commission for your sales.

The hostess is the person who has invited the guests to the party at her home. She will be compensated with free and discounted products. Most companies have hostess programs that allow the hostess to earn free and discounted products for her sales and booking.

The consultant will earn the commissions for the sales and the hostess will earn the free and discounted products for inviting her friends and family over for a fun night. It is a win-win! Both the consultant and the hostess will benefit from the party!

The easiest way for you to get over the fear of calling friends and acquaintances to ask them to host a party is to prepare a script before you call. Once you have written your script, practice it a few times before you dial. Next, stand in front of the mirror and smile at yourself. Yes, I know you will feel silly. You'll probably begin to laugh. Good, now you are ready to call!

When the person you are calling answers identify yourself and affirm why you're calling. You might say, "Hi, Suzy. This is Karen Phelps, and I know it's been a while. But I've joined a new direct selling company." So you're affirming right away—"I know it's been a while, but here's why I'm calling"—instead of acting as if nothing is happening and then all of a sudden saying, "Oh, by the way…" Be up front with the person and let her know why you're calling.

Then share a little something about the company. What is it you love about it or its products? What is your unique selling proposition, (USP) or your thirty-second commercial? What's the reason you joined your company? What is it about the products that interested you and that you want to share with your friend?

The next step is to specify the benefits of being a hostess. If you're calling a friend or an acquaintance, you might want to say to her, "I thought about you because I know you'll love these products. I've been shopping with you and I know how much you like to save on your purchases. When you invite me and a few of your friends over, we'll have a great time and you'll have a substantial savings on your purchase and even receive some product for free."

Now secure the booking. Just say, "So I'm really excited to help you earn some free and discounted products for inviting me and a few friends. I need to hold a party the week of May 3rd and I can work on Tuesday evening or Thursday evening. Which one of those is going to fit best into your schedule?" Don't be afraid to say when you need to hold parties. It's part of your job description! Let's recap.

- ✓ Prepare your script.
- ✓ Smile.
- ✓ Dial.
- ✓ Affirm why you're calling.
- ✓ Share a little bit about your company.
- ✓ Acknowledge the benefits of being a hostess.
- ✓ Secure the booking.

Follow these guidelines and you'll have nothing to be afraid when it comes time to make those first calls.

Create Your Success Calendar

One thing new consultants worry about is if it's possible to work their business around a busy family schedule. We mentioned this earlier, but I wanted to address it in this booking chapter because you are just like other consultants who join because they are looking for a lifestyle-friendly business. Most people already have a family. There are many things happening at home, and you they need to know that the two (business and family) can coexist...if you follow these simple steps:

- ✓ Write any family activities you want to attend on your calendar right away.
- ✓ If you are working a full-time or a part-time job outside the home in addition to your direct selling business, write those hours on the same calendar. Don't have more than one calendar, as you will be headed towards disaster. You need one all-inclusive schedule.

✓ Look at your available timeframes and put a star on the dates you want to schedule your parties.

✓ Schedule time for pre-party and post-party activities. Pre-party activities include hostess coaching, sending out invitations, and talking to your hostess before the party. Most of these activities will be done one to two weeks before the scheduled party. After the party you will need to submit the party orders. You will also want to send a thank-you note to your hostess.

✓ Once your calendar is filled in with things that have to be done, you can begin scheduling other things, like additional phone time, following up on leads, and more family activities.

Once I learned how to schedule my parties using the Open-Date Card system, which is part of my It's A Party Out There program, I discovered the consistency I had been missing my first few years in the business. I now teach people how to control their calendar by taking their thirty-day calendar and transferring the dates they want to work to their Open-Date Card. (You can get a copy of the Open-Date Card from the It's a Party Out There workbook or on the newsletter page of my Web site www.karenphelps.com.) These are the dates you want to hold parties. If when reviewing your calendar you realize you haven't scheduled much time for your business, ask yourself, "Are these the only days I can work, or can I find a few more days to schedule my parties?"

I actively worked this business for twenty-two years, and when I first started I sat down with Larry and said, "When do you want me to schedule my parties?" I knew I was going to need my husband's support to watch the kids while I was gone. He said, "You can work two times a week on Monday through Thursday evenings. I prefer you do not work Friday, Saturdays, and Sundays." I respected his wishes, and to insure his support of my business I did not schedule any parties on weekends. Because I was following our schedule for the business, both of us were happy and content.

It's okay to say no to someone who wants to hold a party on a date that isn't good for you! I know you're afraid she won't hold a party at all if you do this, but I assure you from many years of experience that she will! Ask yourself, "Am I willing to do this party? What will happen if I give in? Am I creating more problems for myself?" Say, for instance, somebody wants to book a party on a Friday night, so you decide do go ahead and hold the party. Most of the people who book from that party will also want to have their party on a Friday evening. Now you develop a pattern of working on days you haven't scheduled to work the business. More people will respect and admire you when you take a firm stand.

It's easy to get what you want. Let people know what you want and expect. At the beginning of each party, explain the advantages and benefits of being in direct selling. I would say, "One of the things I love about having my own direct selling business is I can work around my family schedule. I work Monday through Thursday evenings and I save the weekends for my family because they're my number one priority." Then, when someone approaches you about hosting, they already know there are certain days you are unavailable. If they still approach for a closed-date party, this is a great opportunity to pass a party to a team member. The future hostess will appreciate the flexibility, and the team member will enjoy the opportunity. I personally found it was easier to give up the booking to one of my team members than to do something I didn't want to.

Look for Bookings Everywhere

There is more to being a "Fantastic Booker" than just being organized. You always need to be looking for creative bookings. A creative booking is one you get when you are out networking. Your conversation sparks the desire for the person to want to find out more about your product or hostess opportunity.

Let me take you back to a booking I held in January 1992. I had just finished holding a meeting in a local hotel and was paying for the bill at the front desk. I shared a catalog with front desk clerk, Lisa Santa Cruz, and I explained the benefits for her should she decide to become a hostess. She booked a party. The party was held in January and three more people booked parties of their own.

As an experiment, I decided to track the initial booking. I bought a poster board and wrote her name at the top and the names of three bookings from her party. Every time I got a booking from someone in the chain I wrote their name on the poster. I tracked this chain for over two years! One creative booking created an unbelievable chain! I held 121 parties during the two years, and I sponsored thirteen people into my organization as a result of that one booking. I earned over fourteen thousand dollars in commissions. I eventually ran out of poster space, but the funny thing is the booking chain was still going on. Don't ever ask me, "What difference can one booking make?" If I hadn't followed up with Lisa I would have lost 121 parties, thirteen recruits, and over fourteen thousand dollars in commissions! *Yes*, One booking can make a difference!

You may not know how to approach someone about a booking without getting tongue tied. Well, it's time to create and practice your thirty-second commercial.

✓ What is your unique selling proposition?

✓ What is it that you do?

✓ What do you want to get across to somebody in thirty seconds? If you are with a skin-care company you might say, "I help people look better by providing them with all-natural skin-care." A consultant with a home solutions business could say, "I help people set up organization systems in their home by providing them with storage solutions."

✓ After your thirty-second commercial, ask a question. I found it to be quite easy to give my commercial and then say, "Who do you know that might be interested?"

Never Ask a Yes or No Question

One thing I learned over the years was if I asked, "Would you like to buy something?" or "Would you like to book a party?" my prospect hit the road! People will push back when they feel confronted. If you force someone to make a yes or no decision on the spot the answer will most likely be no. Instead of asking if they are interested, ask, "Who do you know that might be interested in receiving free products just for inviting a few friends and myself over for a fun evening?" By changing the question from "do you?" to "who do you know?" you disarm the person, who will probably respond, "I might be interested. Tell me a little bit more." You can also use the same script for people you already know.

The good news is that you don't have to have the "gift of gab" to do well in this business. In fact, most people talk themselves out of sales and bookings. When people get nervous they tend to talk a lot, and they tend to talk on and on and on. You are much better off having a thirty-second commercial and an important question to follow it up with. What you tell someone in thirty-seconds is building-up for the question. Provide enough information to be interesting, then make it relevant to the individual by asking the question, "Who do you know that might be interested?"

I used to be blatant and bold. I would just ask, "Can I have your name, address, and phone number? I'll send you a catalog." You know what? It was surprising how many people would provide me with their contact information. Since then, I have actually studied another person in the industry, Randy Gage. His suggestion is that, when you're talking to someone, if you want to get their information to call them back, ask them, "Do you have a card?" The natural response will be yes, and you'll have all the information you need. If they don't have a business card, they're likely to say, "Well, no. I don't have a business card, but I can write my name and phone number on a piece of paper for you." After I learned this little secret from Randy Gage, it definitely made a big difference in receiving contact information. That's not to say being bold doesn't work; it worked for me for years, but you'll find that subtlety is often more effective.

Everyone Wants to Know, "What's in It for Me?"

Creating a list of potential hostesses and networking is only part of the process. I cannot stress enough the importance of knowing and understanding your company's hostess program. The hostess program is the plan your company has in place to reward the person who hosts the party. It's important to remember people always want to know, what's in it for me? The person hosting the party (we'll call her hostess) will receive benefits and rewards for inviting her friends and allowing the consultant to demonstrate her products. You company's hostess program could include free as well as discounted products. The hostess program is compensation the company provides the person for inviting you into her home for the party.

The cost of the products supplied to the hostess could be absorbed entirely by the company, or the consultant may be asked to share in the cost of the hostess program. Consultants who are wholesalers, who have inventory products to sell at parties, are usually responsible for the total cost of the products supplied. The hostess may also be asked to pay a small fee as well as tax and shipping on the items she selects. Consultants who must pay a part of the hostess program should consider this a cost of doing business.

The hostess programs provided by each company are as varied as the means to support them. Most companies have a program based on total commissionable sales (not including tax and shipping) for the party. This could also include a larger percentage of free products for more sales. Example: a hostess with three hundred fifty dollars in sales might receive 10 percent for her sales, but when she reaches five hundred dollars in sales the percentage could increase to 15 percent. Increased percentage hostess programs are a great way to motivate the hostess to acquire outside orders to raise the total amount of her party. The program may also include compensation to the hostess who acquires future bookings. The programs vary from half off items immediately to gift certificates to be redeemed at each booking.

You need to know and understand your company hostess program in order to enthusiastically and confidently explain the benefits to the hostess. The easiest way to book parties is by sharing the benefits the hostess will receive when she hosts a party. You may mistakenly believe the hostess will be doing a favor for you when she hosts a party. Your belief is vocalized any time you ask, "Would you like to have a party to help me?" The previous question is placing the focus on you, not the potential hostess or the hostess program.

Offer Everyone the Opportunity to Earn Free and Discounted Products

Now let's change the question a little and see how it sounds. You could say, "Mary, I'd like to offer you to the opportunity to earn some free and discounted products. All you would need to do is invite a few friends over for a fun evening. Our average hostess receives one hundred dollars in free products and two half-off items. I am available on Monday, June 12, or Thursday, June 15. Which of these days is best for you to earn your free and discounted items?" You've turned the tables and are now doing a favor for her. You are willing to help her earn free and discounted products.

You should study the entire hostess program but focus on one of the levels above the company's party average. If the party average for your company is five hundred dollars, you are pretty much going to be guaranteed to have five hundred in sales each time you hold a party.

But you don't want to be average! You want your party average to be higher than the company average. The easiest way to raise your party average is to talk about what a hostess receives for a higher party. If your company's party average is five hundred dollars, then don't talk about the benefits for a hostess at that party level. Talk about the benefits for a hostess who has seven hundred fifty or one thousand dollars in sales. You will increase your party average just by setting the expectation and coaching your hostess to become a seven-hundred-fifty-dollar hostess instead of a five hundred dollar hostess. According to one of my recent surveys, the number one reason over 76 percent of the people who book parties do so is because of what they can earn as a hostess.

Every person you talk to about your company and products wants to know, "What's in it for me? If I use two to three hours of my valuable time, invite my friends into my home, and serve them refreshments, what will I receive for doing this? What is the benefit for me?" With a strong knowledge and belief in your company's hostess program you will never be at a loss for words. The answer will be on the tip of your tongue. Here is an example of what I said to potential hostesses. "Our average hostess receives one hundred fifty dollars in free products, three items for half off, and a hostess-only item when three of her friends book and hold parties. You'll also get me for a few hours of fun! Isn't that exciting?" Okay, I admit it! It sounds corny but everyone laughed, and I did hold an average of three to four parties per week for twenty-two years!

It's always easy for you to book parties when you believe in your company's hostess program. When you believe it is better for someone to spend a few hours of her time, invite her friends and family, enjoy herself, and earn the items she likes for free and discounted prices instead of purchasing them outright, you will never be challenged with booking parties. People will understand you want the best for them. If you are honest with yourself and get out of your own way, you'll be thinking, *Why would anybody want to pay full price when they can earn it for free?* I would look at people who told me they didn't want to have a party and ask, "Are you nuts? Why do you want to pay regular price? Isn't it better to receive some of the items you want free or for a 50 percent discount?" It wasn't difficult for me to ask this question because I really did believe it was a better deal for her to book a party!

Booking Parties Is Easy!

"Asking is the beginning of receiving." —Jim Rohn

You must decide if you want to become an "order taker" or a "booker." An "order taker" will continually have a lack of bookings, whereas a "booker" will always have an abundance of them! When you're part of the direct selling industry, there are several ways to earn money. One of them is selling your products or taking orders and earning a commission on your sales. You most likely do this very well. However, if this is all you do, you will always be looking for creative bookings because you'll leave many parties without any. You will continually be prospecting because your booking calendar is never full.

Once you become a "booker" and you realize the great benefits for each and every hostess; it's like a light bulb turns on and you think to yourself, *I've got to convince these people to book parties because it's for their own best interest.* You quit being just an "order taker" at your parties and begin to focus on offering the opportunity to be a hostess to everyone in attendance. Becoming a "booker" is a change in your mindset.

Don't worry about whether or not there are enough people to book parties. Yes, there is an abundance of people who love to earn free and discounted products! There are many who have never had a home party before, and there are a lot who host two or more each year. There are plenty of people to book, so go ahead and book them!

You can choose to believe there are enough hostesses for everyone or you can begin your business believing there are not enough hostesses for all the consultants in your area. Your booking mentality begins when you first join the business. It can even start without your knowledge. It could begin when your brain processes a negative or positive comment your leader, sponsor, friend, or family member said when you began your direct selling business. The comments you hear at the beginning of your career begin to build your negative or positive beliefs about bookings and other aspects of your business. If someone tells you, "Bookings are hard to get," you will believe it is difficult to obtain bookings.

I was a guest speaker at a meeting and the leader introduced me by saying, "We all know how hard bookings are to get. I brought Karen Phelps in to help us overcome some of the challenges." The leader unknowingly planted a negative thought about bookings. I would rather have been introduced by saying, "This is Karen Phelps. And you know what? Karen believes bookings are easy when you know how. She's joining us tonight to show you how easy it can become for you." So repeat after me, "It's easy to get bookings!"

I'm a Fantastic Booker!

As I drove to my parties over the years I would talk to myself! If you think about it we all talk to ourselves all day long. Most of the time it isn't as positive as it should be. On the way to my parties I would say out loud or to myself, "I'm a fantastic booker. I will go to this party tonight and I will get three bookings." I planted in my mind the results I was expecting to happen. If you have negative thoughts on the way to your parties, begin today to use my booking affirmation. You will soon notice the change in your attitude and your calendar will become full with bookings.

Suggestion: Many successful consultants have told me they won't listen to anything but my CDs on the way to their parties. It gets them in the groove and they are ready to go when they arrive at the party. If you don't have any you can check out the variety of CDs offered on my website at www.karenphelps.com

When a consultant has more bookings than she can hold, she can share the wealth. I learned early in my career that I could have as many bookings as we want. If you believe you can have a lot of bookings, you will have a lot. This frightens some consultants, who do not want to book more parties than they are willing to hold each month. If you can book thirty parties in a month and you only want to hold eighteen, you have several choices you can make.

- You can tell twelve people you are too busy and not book a party with them.
- You can book them two, three, or four months out, which is what most consultants do.
- You can be smart and sponsor some of the hostesses and provide them with the bookings from their party.
- If you are a leader you can give twelve of them to consultants on your team to help them grow their businesses. As a leader, I decided to be the "best booker" on my team. I had so many bookings I never believed consultants who complained, "Nobody wants to book a party." Because I maintained an active booking schedule as a leader, members of my team knew better than to complain about the lack of bookings to me. My abundance of bookings allowed me the opportunity to have a consultant who was struggling observe a party with me and provide her with a few bookings to get her back on track. I was very careful not to let this become

a habit, but as I look back there were several consultants I helped with bookings over the year who went on to become outstanding leaders with our company. I often wonder what would have happened had I not decided to become the "best booker" on my team.

As with anything else, there are hurdles to becoming a "fantastic booker." Some of these hurdles have to do with time. If you begin to feel overwhelmed with too many bookings, go back and reread chapter three. It's important to stay organized with your time so that each party you book will be beneficial for you and the hostess.

Booking is an attitude. Once you decide to do something, whether it's getting someone's contact information, booking parties, or reaching earnings goals, it all becomes simple as long as you *believe it's possible!*

Leader Tip: Work closely with your new recruits during their first six weeks in the business to help them control their calendar and keep their bookings consistent.

Leader Tip: Have everyone on your team create a booking poster of what a hostess can earn when she has a seven hundred and fifty dollar party with three bookings.

What else do you need to do to keep your business growing?

Read on...

CHAPTER FIVE

The Nuts and Bolts to Increase Your Party Profits

A consultant should expect and prepare to book parties from her parties. When you began your business you started with your warm market. These are the people you know, which include friends, family and all of the people who booked your initial parties. You must have systems in place and be prepared to book parties from every party to replace your initial bookings and grow your business. You also need to ask all your hostesses for referrals.

You have your contact list and you've made calls. Some people said, "Yes, I'm going to book a party from you," and others said, "No, not at this time." Let's assume you made twenty phone calls and seven people said they would host a party and thirteen people told you no. You need to be prepared to ask the thirteen people who told you "no" for a referral. If someone says no, say, "I understand you aren't interested right now and thank you for taking the time to talk to me. Who do you know that might be interested in getting some of these products for free?" If you don't ask for a referral, you'll never get a referral. Be prepared to ask.

Ask for Referrals

"The best time to ask for a referral is when you have just made the sale or held the party." —Karen Phelps

I learned my lesson about the importance of referrals from my insurance agent. When we were first married we had a great insurance man, and every two years he would come to our home to review our policy with us. He wanted to see if we needed to update it or increase the amount of life insurance, especially after we purchased our home and had children. When he was done talking to us, Bill always asked, "Okay, we are done protecting you and your family. Now who do you know who could benefit from the same type of coverage you have?" After he said this he made no attempt to leave, and we knew he wasn't going to leave the house if we didn't get him some referrals. My husband, Larry, has much more patience than I do and is the type of person who would have sat there forever, but I would begin to get a little antsy and eventually I'd go and get my address book and provide him with three or four referrals. I'm not sure if any of them purchased insurance from him, but it was easier to provide him with names than it was to house and feed him for a week, which I was pretty sure would happen if I didn't go along with his request.

So ask people and then look at them as if you expect them to give you referrals. Bill was very good with the way he posed the question. "Who else do you know who could benefit from the type of benefits you are receiving from your insurance?" I learned that if you don't ask, you won't receive.

You need to get people fired up. You have to be careful when you say something like, "Everyone seems burned out on home parties. No one wants to have one." Everyone's not burned out on home parties. There may be a few people who are because they may be part of a group that has a lot of home parties. Someone might say, "Oh, no. Not another home party." Ask yourself, "What is it that makes my product different than the other products sold at home parties?" When you call your friend and she says, "There have been so many home parties going on in our area, I really don't know," you can say, "You know what? This is different." You might ask her, "What type of home parties have you been to in the past few months?" Take time to explain what makes your product different and reveal the savings she will receive as a hostess.

When a consultant on my team had difficulty acquiring bookings from her warm leads in the beginning or after she'd been in the business for a while, I encouraged her to stop by and visit her friends rather than call on the phone. I told her to call and say, "Hey, I'd like to stop by. Do you have ten or fifteen minutes in the next day or two? I want to stop by and show you some products." If she resists, offer to bring a dessert or coffee from your favorite coffee shop—we all find it hard to resist free dessert and coffee! By using this method she booked and additional six parties.

Rather than calling and trying to convince someone over the phone—especially if she doesn't know anything about your product—

show up with a few of your products (and dessert and coffee). Don't forget to bring a Hostess Packet with you. You can do a mini-demonstration of your products for her. Explain some of the qualities and features of the products. Have her browse the catalog and select some of the things she likes. Then say, "Let me show you how you can have a substantial savings on the items you like by hosting a party and inviting me and few friends into your home." Show her the savings!

Begin Planting Booking Seeds Immediately

Once you arrive at the party, you must begin planting booking seeds immediately. A booking seed is a subliminal suggestion. It subconsciously provides people with reasons to become a hostess. You must continually plant seeds as to what they will receive when they host a party.

You could begin your presentation with a question. One of the questions asked at every party was, "How many of you've ever had any type of home party before? Raise your hand." I raised my right hand, and by asking one simple question, I planted my first booking seed. Through a show of hands I found out the people who had hosted some type of home party before and who were not resistant to the idea of having one. It's amazing what you can find out when you *ask*!

When you provide your hostess with her thank-you gift, you could also say, "Here is your thank-you gift. Thank you so much for hosting a party for me." This is another booking seed. When you demonstrate one of the most popular items, you can point out that it is the kind of product your company thanks its hostesses with, whether for free or at deep discount. You could say, "This is one of our most popular items and a lot of our hostesses love to select this item as one of their half-off items." Voila, you have just planted another booking seed!

It's the little suggestions during the course of your presentation that get people thinking about the benefits should they become a hostess.

You can book more parties at a home party than any other time. The guests in attendance at your party will see, smell, touch, and fall in love with the products. There's a benefit to seeing the physical product rather than viewing it in a catalog. You probably already have observed guests purchasing more of the items you demonstrate in your kit than other items in the catalog. The product you sell may be one that is much more beautiful in person than in the catalog. You may have to demonstrate products and show guests how they work. The guests get caught up in the excitement of the party and friends shopping together and for each other. They are having fun. That's why they call it a party! It doesn't matter whether your company calls them shows, classes, lessons, or anything else. It will be a party if you make it fun.

Another reason that people book more parties from a home party is because they understand and have visualized the reward and seen the benefits to the hostess. They believe, *This is a good deal for me. I can give up a few hours of my time, invite my friends, enjoy myself, and earn these products at a substantial savings.* During the party, you must make sure the guests understand the hostess program. You must talk about the hostess program at least three times during every home party. Be specific. It goes right back to knowing and understanding your company's hostess program, but having one increment you want to focus on, which is above the company's party average. If you want a seven-hundred-fifty-dollar party and three bookings, talk about what a hostess will receive when she has a seven-hundred-fifty-dollar party and three bookings *at least three times during the party.*

Again, I cannot stress enough the importance of being specific rather than vague. If I was a guest at your party and you said, "You can earn free and discounted items," that would mean nothing to me. If you said, "Our hostesses earn an average of one hundred fifty dollars in free product and three half-price items," I would immediately understand what I would receive as a hostess.

Create a Visual Demonstration of Your Hostess Program

There are many ways to do this. You can do a visual demonstration of your hostess program. Choose a guest who arrives early and ask her to look at the catalog or your samples to select some of her favorite items. Use the items she selected and figure out on a notecard how much she would pay as a guest, how much she would pay as a hostess, and what her total savings are. During the party demonstrate the savings she will receive when she books a home party. Use the items she selected to demonstrate the hostess program by stacking them on her lap. You could say, "Mary selected these items as some of her favorites. Let me show you how much you can save when you invite me and a few friends over for a fun party."

After you have completed the demonstration of your products, review the hostess program. This is an important step that can dramatically increase the amount of bookings you get at every party. When you begin your party and explain the company's hostess program, many guests are not embracing the idea of having a party, as they haven't seen the product and so don't know if they're interested. After you've completed your demonstration and the guests fall in love with what they've seen, you recap what they can receive as a hostess. Now they have a reason to book! They've seen several items they like and they are willing to trade time for money. A few hours as a hostess can often save them several hundred dollars!

Coach Your New Hostesses to Success

Once you've booked parties you need to prepare your hostess for what she needs to do to have a successful party. The absolute best time to coach your hostess is immediately when she schedules her party. Once a guest has expressed an interest in hosting a party, it is imperative for you to agree on a date and provide her with a hostess packet. If she is in attendance and books while she is at a home party, provide her with her hostess packet and coach her before she leaves. If the potential hostess is not at a home party or if it is someone you've called on the phone, you must first agree on a date for her party, let her know you'll call in a few days, and then mail her hostess packet to her. You should explain what she will need to do at the initial time of booking and then call her a few days later to make sure the hostess packet has arrived. On the follow-up call after she has her hostess packet, review the contents with her and remind her of all the important things she will need to do in order to have a successful party to maximize her hostess rewards

There are four important steps to hostess coaching. The first which we previously mentioned is securing a date that will work for both you and the hostess. If you don't have a date, you don't have a booking! The second step is to provide her with the hostess packet and review the contents of the hostess packet with her. When coaching your hostess you must also let her know what she needs to do. I've found it easy to have a simple checklist, which I created on the computer that gives her five simple steps.

1. Over-invite; try to invite at least twenty people.
2. Return guest lists to me within three days.
3. Get at least four orders before the party.
4. Call guests to remind them to come and bring a friend.
5. Keep refreshments simple.

Providing a hostess with a simple list of things to do will help keep her from becoming overwhelmed before her party. Having a party should be fun and rewarding for the hostess. Keeping your hostess packet and coaching simple will help her maintain enthusiasm for her upcoming party.

Take time to send out a "thank you for booking" note. I liked to mail the hostess a special note the day after she decides on a date for her party. You can create a form letter or flyer on the computer, but if you do, keep it simple. Don't write too much. We have become such a high-tech society that you may be tempted to just send an e-mail—and by all means, that is better than nothing. But just imagine how important your new hostess will feel if you take time to write a personal thank-you note. It is so out of the normal now that you will stand out from the crowd. You can use a simple thank-you card and write on the inside, "I want to thank you for booking a party. I'm looking forward to helping you receive the items you have on your wish list. Please remember to return your guest list to me in three days."

If you do not receive the guest list within three days you will need to make a call for her guest list to insure you can mail her invitations out on time.

Increase the Attendance at Your Home Parties

You can substantially increase your chances of making sure the parties that are scheduled hold when you mail out the invitations for the hostess. When you receive the guest list back from the hostess, which is part of her homework, you will then send out the invitations for her. I mailed invitations for my hostesses for over twenty-two years and my cancellation and postponement rate was less than five percent, which is very, very good for the industry. Taking responsibility for mailing the invitations will make it much easier on the hostess. She will provide you with a list of the people she would like to invite to her party. Your company may have a hostess guest list available for you, but if not, check out the "Hostess Triplicate Guest Lists" available at www.karenphelps.com. Besides having a better chance of your scheduled party holding, there are a few other advantages of receiving a list and mailing invitations for your hostess. These include knowing how many guests are invited to the party, knowing exactly when the invitations were mailed out, and having a duplicate list that can be used when the hostess rebooks another party.

As a rule of thumb, the invitations should be mailed at least seven days but not more than fourteen days before the party. The exception to this is if the hostess books a party that is within seven days, in which case ask your hostess to call her guests first and then use the invitations as a reminder. Remind her to call the people who were invited that she has not yet heard from. The personal reminder calls from the hostess can increase the amount of guests who attend, and of course, the more guests in attendance the higher the sales.

Many companies are embracing new technology and sending e-mail invitations. These can be perceived as less personal and more easily dismissed by those who are invited to the party. The increase of spam filters also makes it challenging for us to know if the people invited received their invitations. Using e-mail reminders can be very effective when they follow up a mailed invitation, and they can be sent quickly and effortlessly by you or the hostess. The more your hostess follows up with invited guests the greater her chance of having a successful party.

When you mail the invitations to the guests, also mail an invitation to the hostess with a follow up letter, which might read, "The invitations to your party have been mailed and your guests should be receiving them within a few days. Please call your guests to remind them to come and to bring a friend." If you decide not to mail a follow-up letter then send your hostess an e-mail stating the same thing. When using e-mail follow up make sure you request a "read receipt" so you will know the hostess has received the e-mail.

The third step to hostess coaching is your hostess reminder call. A follow-up phone call to your hostess three to four days before the party will help you know how many people she has coming, and you can give her some suggestions for pulling it all together so she can have a successful party and earn maximum benefits as a hostess.

After the party is complete and the guests have received their purchases, you will need to do some more follow up; which is the fourth step in hostess coaching. It doesn't matter whether everyone receives their products at the time of the party or whether they have been delivered or mailed to the hostess; when all of the guests who purchased have received their orders you need to make sure everyone is satisfied. Call your hostess and answer her questions and make sure everything is okay. Providing good service for your hostess will increase your chances of booking her for another party at a later date.

Create Customer Loyalty

When you take time to follow up with the guests who were in attendance, especially the guests who placed good orders but did not book a party, you have the chance to get more bookings. During the call you can thank the guest for her order and offer the opportunity to become a hostess. If you take time before the call to see what she purchased, you could suggest additional items she may want to add. Your conversation could go like this: "Hi, Melissa, this is Karen and I want to thank you for attending Sally's party and placing an order. I noticed you purchased several items that were part of a group. There are a couple other pieces that would go very nicely with this. Would you be interested in earning these for free?" Often the guest is not ready to book the night she's at the home party, but when you follow up two or three weeks later she realizes she would really like to have some additional items. Your follow-up phone call could result in an additional order or a booking on your calendar.

You want your hostess and your guests to remember you when they want additional products or they want to book a party. Make sure everyone has your business card, or better yet a magnet with your name, phone number, e-mail address, and Web site. Make sure everyone knows how they can contact you. Keep your name in front of your hostesses and guests all the time.

When a new catalog is released, make sure your good hostesses and customers receive one from you as soon as possible. You can also let them know about a new online catalog, but from my personal experience I spend much less time looking at catalogs online while it's easy for me to browse through three or four while I'm watching a favorite show on television. The longer you're in business, the more repeat hostesses you will have. You will quickly learn what they like and what some of their favorite items are.

When a new catalog comes out and you see a few items a past hostess might like, take time to call her. You could say, "Hey, Suzie, this is Karen. I'm so excited. We have a new catalog and there are a couple items that as soon as I saw them I thought of you. You'll love them and I want to help you earn them for free. I have available dates for a party, so let's find one that will work so you can earn these new items." Talk to her about the opportunity to be a hostess, and if she's not interested right then let her know you will drop off or mail a catalog to her; even if she doesn't book she may still place an order.

Technology is great. When I think back to the times when I spent hours creating a flyer and mailing it to hostesses and customers, I often wonder how I got it all done. You can and should continue to do some direct mailing to hostesses because a personally addressed envelope produces the highest response. Now we also have the advantage of sending mass electronic newsletters to our hostesses and customers. There are many great e-mail systems and solutions you can use to create a newsletter for your hostesses and customers. Keeping everyone informed on a monthly basis will help you build better relationships. These electronic newsletters could list current monthly hostess and customer specials, as well as a few tips and suggestions on how to use something in the catalog. Your company may already have an e-mail system set up through your individual Web site, but if not there are several good electronic e-mail sources available. Monthly newsletters and periodic mailings will keep your business growing and your customers returning to you.

Leader Tip: Show new consultants how to demonstrate the host rewards at their parties.

Leader Tip: Role play with new consultants how to effectively hostess coach.

What is the single most important thing you can do to grow your direct selling business?

Read on...

CHAPTER SIX

Unravel the Mystery of Sponsoring

My definition of sponsoring is *"an unselfish act of sharing a fantastic opportunity."* You don't have to sponsor; however, when you understand what sponsoring really is you will want to.

The first reason you will want to sponsor is because you want to share something good! When you discover something fantastic you want to share your discovery with others. Think about the last time you went to the theatre and saw a good movie. The next day you probably called your friends and said, "Oh, my gosh. I just saw the greatest movie and you have to go see it!" That's exactly what happens when you discover a great business opportunity. You want to share it with everybody.

The second reason you will want to sponsor is to increase your earnings. When you are with a direct selling company, the advantage of bringing people into the business is compensation. You will receive some type of incentive for bringing other people in. You may receive compensation for bringing others into the company, as well as credit towards company incentives and contests.

The third reason you will want to sponsor is to earn a different status or to be promoted to a leadership level within your company. Most likely you will also receive additional compensation as you move up the leadership ladder.

It's certainly possible for a consultant to join your team who doesn't want to sponsor anyone else. She may be working her business very part-time or she may be uncomfortable in a leadership position. That's okay; you can still encourage her and help teach her what to do if somebody approaches her who is interested in joining.

You may have decided you do not want to sponsor, which is your prerogative. But never turn someone down or prevent them from starting their own business. If you aren't interested in sponsoring, have your leader or another consultant contact the prospective new consultant. If you've made the decision not to sponsor anyone, take time to speak to your leader so when this happens to you, you have a plan in place.

Sponsoring Is a Way to Help Others

If you want to sponsor, a very easy way for consultants to get their first recruit is to identify friends and family members that could use extra income. When you joined, you probably thought to yourself, *Carol could use some additional monthly income.* You probably thought of a friend, family member, or somebody else who would be good in the business. It could be someone who loves the type of product you are selling, or she could be a natural "people person," somebody who would be a good consultant. A great place to start is with your warm market. Who amongst your friends and family might be interested, and who would be good in this business?

You don't have to wait until you are successful in the business before you can begin sponsoring others. One of the great benefits of joining a direct selling company is that you have so many others, like your sponsor and your upline leaders, who are going to help you when you begin sponsoring. Your new recruit could be going through training at the same time you are. There's no reason to wait until you're successful to start sponsoring. The longer you wait to begin to sponsor, the less likely sponsoring will become natural for you. The longer you take to begin sponsoring, the harder it will be to develop the habits you need to do in order to find people and bring them into your business.

Be very careful not to prejudge. You may have a specific type of person you are looking for who you feel will be the ideal consultant. This single-mindedness could cost you many recruits. You may only be looking for stay-at-home moms who are of a certain age and ignore someone who is totally opposite but could be your next recruit.

As I mentioned in the beginning of this book, there is no "perfect fit" when it comes to direct selling. There are so many different types and ages of people in direct selling, and we have to be careful not to stereotype and prejudge. Personally, my best recruit ever was the person at my party who I thought least likely to be interested in the business. When I first met her at a party I was pretty intimidated by her; she struck me as someone who was not in need of the money and not really looking for a business. She was very friendly, though, and loved the product, and when she told me she wanted to sell, I almost fell off my chair. She went on to become a very successful leader with our company. I often wonder what would have happened if she hadn't asked me about selling.

I learned a very valuable lesson that night: always approach the person who intimidates you the most. We often have blinders on and look for one type of person that's going to fit this perfect mold that we have. That's not always what real life is going to bring to us. You must be open-minded. You need to share the benefits of what your company has to offer, and then by asking questions and observing people, find those who may be interested in finding out more.

Hostesses Make Great Consultants

The easiest person to sponsor at your home parties is the hostess. She is someone who is already sold on the benefits of your products and has booked a party because she wants to profit from the sales. When you are hostess coaching her, you might want to say something like, "Have you ever thought about doing something like this?" You can talk to your hostess several times, when you first coach her and then again when you make that little follow-up phone call. After the party you can talk to the hostess and say, "Have you thought any more about doing this? I think you'd be absolutely phenomenal. And, oh, by the way, you watched what I did. You saw how easy this was. Do you realize you could have earned one hundred fifty dollars tonight for a couple hours? Could you use one hundred fifty dollars a couple times a week?" Stop talking and wait for her reply. She might want more information or she might not be interested at all. The important thing to remember is to ask every hostess if she is interested in the business opportunity.

To spark interest in the business opportunity, you should tell your story. You have to keep this brief; it should take no longer than to two to three minutes to tell why you joined your company. A ten or fifteen-minute monologue about why you're doing the business will bore your guests to tears. All you need is a very short explanation of why you joined your company, the benefits, and what you enjoy about it. When you're telling your story, use other people as examples. You might say, "If you're a stay-at-home mom and you could earn some additional income, this might be for you. Or if you're a single mom who needs a little extra cash at the end of the month, this could be the answer for you. If you're a working mother and you'd like to have a way to stay home with your kids, this might be the answer for you. If you're a retiree and you need extra income once you retire so you can live the lifestyle you want, this could be the answer for you." Your story is a combination of why you're doing this, as well as why other people look at your company's opportunity as a solution to their challenge.

One of the easiest ways for consultants to promote the business opportunity at their parties is the sponsoring game. This game is explained in my It's A Party Out There workbook, which you can find at www.karenphelps.com. For the first twelve years in my business, I did not play games. Yes, I admit, I was not a person who liked to play games! I was so resistant to playing games that I hesitate to call this a game now, in case your thinking was like mine used to be. The sponsoring game is a nonthreatening way of providing your guests with the information they need about the business opportunity. During the first part of the sponsoring game, you will allow the guests to ask you questions about your business and you will provide them with the answers.

One guest may ask you, "How much does it cost to get started?" and you will respond with a thirty-second answer. The game in the It's A Party Out There workbook consists of the basic eight questions and answers that will provide the guests with the most information about your business. The basic principle of this game it to keep the information simple and short in order to pique curiosity in the some of the guests.

The second part of the sponsoring game is comprised of questions you will ask the guests to help you discover why they might be interested in the business opportunity. These are a few of the questions you will ask during the second part of the sponsoring game.

1. What do you do? Where do you work? Do you work outside the home? Part-time, full-time?

2. If you had an extra one thousand dollars a month, what would you spend it on?

3. What intrigues you about having your own business with our company, and would you like some more information?"

4. Would you like more information on how you can earn the extra one thousand dollars per month?

The sponsoring game was a major contributing factor to the amount of new recruits brought into our organization. Everyone who was a part of our team learned how to play it as part of their initial training. The simplicity of the game allowed new consultants to overcome their initial fear of sponsoring. When you implement the sponsoring game into your presentation, you will discover there are many people in attendance at your home parties who are interested in finding out about the business opportunity. You will learn to offer the opportunity to more people.

Your company most likely has a sponsoring brochure that includes information about the business opportunity. When someone expresses an interest in the business, you will send them home with a catalog and sponsoring information provided by your company. You also will want to set an appointment for a follow-up phone call to answer any questions. The follow-up call will be used to set an interview appointment, which will allow you to provide the person with more information in a personal setting. It is much better not to try to explain how to get started while on the telephone unless your prospect lives too far for you to meet with personally. The more information you provide on the telephone the harder it is to close. Your prospect may tell you she wants to think about it, and you could lose the opportunity to find out what is preventing her from joining.

You need to discover why she is interested in the opportunity, not just why the opportunity would be good for her. You need to find out her wants and needs in order to have an effective close. As soon as you just begin telling people, "Oh, this would be good for you," you are putting them into a mold. You're trying to fit them into something that might not be the perfect fit for them.

Questions Are the Answer

Ask more questions. Instead of talking and explaining how to get started as soon as you begin the conversation, ask questions. Begin with personal questions like, "Tell me a little bit about yourself. Are you married? Are you single? How many kids do you have? Are your kids still at home?" Find out a little bit about your prospect. Beginning with the first question you ask her, each of her answers provides you with the next question. So if she says, "Yes, I'm married," you say, "How many children do you have?" She replies, "Two." You answer, "That's how many I have, too. What ages are your children?" She will she then tell you their ages. You could follow up with, "Have you worked outside the home before? Do you work outside the home right now?" And if she says, "Yes, I work outside the home," you ask, "Do you work full-time or part-time?" You are the one asking questions—and remember, every answer she gives you is providing you with the next question.

You then try to discover why she is interested in the business opportunity by asking more questions. Your next question could be, "If you had an extra thousand dollars a month, what would you do with it?" She answers, "I would really like to really take my family on a vacation." "Oh, really? Where would you like to go?" She says, "I'd like to take the kids to Disney World." "When do you want to go?"

You begin having a conversation! When you are done asking questions, you've found out what she wants the income for. *You know you have a solution for her, and now you have your close!* You'll say, "So if I could show you how you could make an extra one thousand dollars a month to set aside to take your family on a vacation to Disney World and work the business during the times you have available, would you like to find out more?"

> *"Before you state your case, gather the evidence, especially what motivates the other person." —Denis Waitley*

The more questions you ask, the easier it will be for you to find a reason for people to meet with you to hear about your business opportunity. You need to ask as many questions as you can to get you to the point where you can wrap it up and deliver it back in a way that makes it impossible for her to not want more information. There are no set questions, and there are not a certain number of questions you need to ask each time. Your choice of questions is what is most important. When you are done asking questions you should know *why would this person be interested in our business opportunity and why is this business opportunity the perfect solution for her?*

The important thing to remember is that once you have sparked an interest in the prospective recruit and sent her home with some information about your company, you always want to get to the next step. At the initial contact provide her with information and set a time for a follow-up phone call. During the follow-up phone call, the next step is to sit down with her to explain how easy it is to get started in the business. When you meet with her, the next step is to get a signed agreement or a no. Once a prospect is added to your list of people to contact you need to follow through until you get a yes or no.

It's Time to Schedule an Interview

You might be sending leads to your company's website as part of your follow up. While this can work once in a while, the method that will provide you with the best results is the face-to-face interview. When you meet with someone over a cup of coffee or lunch, you have the ability to watch the person's body language. You will not only hear what she is saying to you, you will watch her movements as she is talking.

Observing someone while you are speaking is a great way to know if they are comfortable with you and with the questions. If you notice she is not relaxed, you can assume a more relaxed posture to help put her at ease. Everything you hear and everything you see helps you to know how to close that person. You need to discover what may be stopping her from joining or preventing her from seeing this as a possible solution for her. When you take the time to do face-to-face interviews, you will definitely increase your closing ratio.

There are basic steps for interviewing a prospect about the business opportunity. The first step is to ask questions. Here are a few you might try:

- What impressed you at the home party?
- What impressed you about the products?

- What was it that you liked most about the products?
- How much money would you like to earn from this business per week?
- What do you want to spend the money on?
- How much time can you devote to your business per week?
- How many parties would you like to hold per week?
- Should you decide to do this, how much time could you invest in the business?

Definitely begin the interview by asking questions. You may already know some of the answers from previous contact, but there might be other questions you would like to ask to help you better understand what she expects from the business.

The second part of the interview is your chance to explain how to get started with your company. You can provide information about the kit she will receive after signing up, the process of signing up, and the cost to join. You need to explain step by step how to get started with your company. During the information part of the interview make sure to explain the various ways to earn money with your company including a few membership levels. During your presentation of the company compensation program you can stop and ask her, "Do you see yourself eventually becoming a leader with our company?"

For the third part of the interview you need a closing question that will get "Yes I want to join" or "No, I'm not interested in joining." There are several different closes. This was my favorite closing question: "If I agree to teach you and give you all the information you need, do you think you could do a good job with this?" If she said yes, I replied, "Great, how would you prefer to pay for your kit?" I would get an agreement or registration form and have her begin to fill it in. The reason I loved using that question is because it begins the closing with a *yes* question. For over twenty years I have never had anyone say, "No, I couldn't do a good job." They may have a question or an objection, and if they do, answer it and then proceed.

It doesn't matter what question you use to close as long as you use something. Even if you have to ask, "Do you want to join?" you cannot leave an interview not knowing whether the person wants to join. You don't want a "Let me think about it" or "I might be interested." You want to get a yes or no so you can move on to the next prospect.

Once your prospect has said yes and completes her agreement and provides you with payment, you need to let her know what she needs to begin working on immediately. Encourage her and remind her that if she follows the steps you are providing, she will begin realizing success within her first thirty days. This will put her one step closer to her earnings goal.

Leader Tip: Teaching your team to use the Sponsoring Game, which is part of the It's a Party Out There program will help your new recruits begin sponsoring within their first months in the business!

Leader Tip: Show new consultants how to effectively hold interviews by taking them along with you when you meet with their prospective recruits.

Do you want to just recruit – or do you want to build a direct selling empire?

Read on...

CHAPTER SEVEN

Uncover the Secret of How to Build a Team to Multiply Your Earnings

You can really help your new recruit succeed in the business when you take time to find out her goals at the interview, or when she says, "Yes, I want to become a consultant." The sooner you find out what your new recruit's goals are, the easier it will be for you to work with the consultant and get her moving in the right direction.

Expect Your New Recruits to Succeed

In the previous chapter I mentioned that you should let the new recruit know what she needs to begin working on immediately. You need to assign homework at the interview. Inform her right away of the things she needs to do to get her business started on the fast track to success.

It's easy to get someone to do things as long as you also remind her that your purpose is to help her to succeed and reach her goals. I used to say, "Your first thirty days are going to be both busy and exciting. You'll be learning how to do the business, and holding your open-for-business party and your first parties. I'm going to help you begin earning right away."

It will help if you bring a calendar or datebook for the next sixty days so you can begin to enter things as you discuss them. These are a few of the things you should have your new recruit begin working on immediately.

- Set a date for her open-for-business party. Don't leave the interview without a tentative date for this very important party. The longer the new consultant takes to begin her business, the longer it will take for her to begin earning from the business.

- Provide her with dates for her training. Will the training be with a group or one-on-one? Will the training be on the phone? Your new consultant needs to know how and when she will receive training.

- Provide her with several dates for her to come and observe parties. Let her select at least one and preferably two dates to observe. These dates could be for observing your parties or another consultant's or leader's parties. This on-the-job training is a great way to model the things your new consultant needs to do at each party to maximize results. Observation parties shouldn't be a matter of choice for a new consultant, and consultants who want to succeed will do what is recommended.

- Help your consultant decide when she wants to hold her parties and mark these dates on her calendar. You can then transfer them to an Open-Date Card for her. When she begins calling her friends to get her initial bookings, she will begin filling her calendar with bookings on her first available dates.

- Have the new recruit call you within forty-eight hours with her first four to six bookings.

Within forty-eight to seventy-two hours the new consultant should already have some type of training with the person who sponsored her into the business. It could be a telephone training where you review the company fast-start or quick-start guide. You want to review the simple steps to success for her first thirty days. Don't let your new recruit go more than seventy-two hours without a phone call from you. The more contact you have with her initially the greater her chances for success. Your job is to continually keep her moving in the direction of her goals.

Begin to inspect the homework you assigned at the interview. Are things beginning to happen or has your new recruit stalled? Has she set the open-for-business party? Does she have her list ready for the people she wants to invite? Have the invitations been mailed for the party? Has she attended one or two observation parties? When your children have homework, as a parent, you inspect and make sure they get it done. The same is true with your new recruits. You are the person giving the homework assignments. You must check to insure everything is moving forward and the assignments are being completed so she can realize the success she wants from the business.

A new consultant will be very excited and anxious, and she will probably call her sponsor or leader every day. She will have questions and concerns, especially as her first party approaches. The first six weeks in the business are crucial to a new consultant's success. During these first six weeks, besides answering the questions she has when she calls, you will want to follow up with her after every party she holds. After the new consultant has been in the business for six or seven weeks, you'll find she is calling you less often. You might only be talking to her once a week, and this is okay as long as she knows you are available to answer any of her questions.

People Want to Be Held Accountable

"Leadership is the capacity to translate vision into reality." —Warren G. Bennis

A recent survey that I conducted found that the number one reason people wanted me to coach them was they wanted to be held accountable to reach their goals. Leaders are often afraid to hold people accountable because we don't want them to resist, and yet these people are saying, "When somebody holds me accountable, I actually achieve more." Learn from this and always remind your new recruits of your goal to help them succeed.

You need to have an easy-to-duplicate system to use at your parties if you are going to use them as a way to train your new recruits. When a new recruit observes you doing a party, you should be doing all the things you need to do to get sales, bookings, and recruit leads. When you have a system in place, you don't have to think about it. You don't have to wonder, *Did I do this, did I mention that?* More importantly, the new recruits you're training at your parties will observe you doing all the things you've told her to do at her home parties.

The best time to approach a new recruit about becoming a leader is at the interview. During the interview, after I had explained how to get started, reviewed the kit options and gone through a little bit of the business opportunity, I let the prospect know the benefits of sponsoring people into the business and how she could easily become a leader with our company. When I reached that part of my presentation, I would pause, look at the person I was interviewing, and say, "This is how to move up in our company. Do you see yourself eventually becoming a leader with our company?" And I would wait for her to answer. The ironic thing is, by asking the question, most people responded, "Yes, I do see myself becoming a leader." You can easily plant the idea of becoming a leader at the interview and then nurture it down the road.

A good way to identify potential leaders is by gauging their desire to work their own business. If they don't attack their own priorities with everything they have, then there's no reason to expect them to give one hundred percent to someone else. You want to look for someone with a good attitude, and someone who doesn't make excuses. A consultant who says, "I can't find anyone who wants to host a party," will have a hard time teaching others how to get bookings. She might be having a bad day when she says this and she may be a great consultant, but this isn't the example a leader should be providing for her team.

Potential Leaders Are Everywhere

You can identify potential leaders by working with somebody who is already sponsoring. Someone who has already sponsored one or two people into your company is a great candidate. Look for someone who is supportive, someone who is already helping other people. If you've identified somebody you see as a potential leader, who hasn't told you she is interested in becoming a leader, ask her if she's interested. Maybe you have someone who has sponsored a person already and you ask her, "Are you interested in becoming a leader?" If she says yes, invite her to a special training.

There is a very simple program to multiply the number of leaders on your team. Hold a "future leader luncheon" or meeting every month. I held a future leader luncheon once a month and invited people who wanted to find out how to become leaders, or others whom I believed could be leaders. You need to establish a system or process for finding and developing leaders. It doesn't make sense to keep going back to square one every time you find a candidate.

A future leader can begin training and working with her own recruits as soon as she feels comfortable in the knowledge she has gained. Somebody may already have previous experience in direct selling. She will be more comfortable training people than others who do not have any previous experience in direct selling. As soon as she learns the new company's systems and procedures, she can begin to train her own people.

If you are a new future leader and you don't feel comfortable about training your recruits, make sure you're working with your leader to acquire the skills and confidence you need. As soon as you feel comfortable enough to begin training your new recruits, say, "I'm ready to start training my recruits, but just in case I need you, you'll be there for me, right?" Don't alienate your leaders. Your leaders are there to help and support you. Knowing your leader will still be there to help and support you is like having a safety net underneath you. You're going to begin to work on your own, but should you have any questions, you want to make sure she's there to help you.

A leader should expect her future leaders to support her in the things she has going on for her team. The easiest way to increase their chances for success is to involve them immediately in some of the activities you have going on. The best compliment you can give someone is to show them you believe in them by allowing them to teach. It doesn't work if you teach people how to do things but then don't allow them to do them. This is especially true with leaders. We teach them the skills they need to do the interviews and train their new recruits, but we don't trust them enough to let them do it.

So, I repeat, the best compliment you can pay someone is to allow them to get out on their own and begin teaching and training their team. By doing this you're saying, "I believe in you. I believe that you can do this. Now go out there and just get it done. Start training your people. You can do it."

Build a Support System

"Relationships are the glue that holds team members together." —John Maxwell

Being a dominant "type A" this was particularly hard for me. I wanted to do everything myself. I was the person who thought, *I have to do this because this is the only way it's going to get done right.* It created a little friction early on with some other strong-willed people I brought into the business. They had become leaders but I was not allowing them to act as leaders. I learned that by my micromanaging them, I was basically saying, "I don't trust you enough. You've brought these people into the business, and, yes, you're a leader, but I don't trust that you're going to do it right." It was a hard lesson for me to learn. I had to learn to teach and let go, to allow them to do their own thing but know I was there if they needed me.

As you bring people into this business, you watch them grow. It's exactly like watching your children grow up. You nurture them when they are new to the business. You teach them the nuts and bolts so they have the education and everything they need to become successful. Once they have grown and become independent, they leave the nest.

You develop a leader and soon she is strong enough to leave. She says, "I'm ready. I'm going to start doing things on my own." You will most likely have mixed emotions about the release of your newly developed leader. You are excited to have helped her reach her new status, but you're also sad to see her go off on her own. She will be leaving you and your team to work on building and developing her own. You should feel very proud. You look back at the hard work, the love, the sweat, the tears, and everything that goes into helping someone become a strong leader, and you begin to think, *I was a part of this. I helped this person move forward on the road to success.*

There are several things leaders can do to create the desire for others on the team to want to become leaders. The first thing is to always demonstrate your company's compensation or marketing program. A leader needs to create opportunities to talk about how to move up to leadership within her company. You need to talk about the marketing program and all the advantages of becoming a leader at every meeting and training.

The second thing you want do is minimize complaining. I was in the business long enough to know there will always be challenges. As leaders, we have to be very careful who we are talking to. We don't ever want to complain downwards. As soon as we begin complaining to consultants on our team, they begin to look at our position and say, "Oh, I don't think I want to be a leader because I don't want to deal with that." I always teach people to send their complaints up and their compliments down.

The third thing you want do is to maximize the potential earnings. Show your team how they can earn more money by moving up. You want to minimize the work that goes into leadership and maximize the results they're going to get. You should always talk about the potential earnings, the benefits, the other rewards, the contests and prizes they can earn. Focus on the results of being a leader.

Leader Tip: Have a training system outline which will be used by all members of your team when training new consultants.

What do you have
to do to provide your
team with the attitudes,
skills and knowledge
they need to solve
their own problems?

Read on...

CHAPTER EIGHT

Learn How to Become a "Superstar Leader"

"You must manage yourself, before you can lead anyone else." —Zig Ziglar

Friendly, enthusiastic, outgoing people make great leaders, but successful leaders realize it's not about them; it's about their people.

Being a good leader is a lot like being a good parent. You need to set expectations and you need to set an example. Good leaders do things others don't want to do. Good leaders expect results others don't believe they can get. Good leaders aren't afraid to tell someone they can do better. Let's begin with setting expectations for our recruits.

If you are a consultant or leader who struggles with getting your new recruits to attend training classes, the easiest thing you can do is to ask your new recruit at the interview, "Can you set aside a couple hours a week for continued training your first month in the business?" You have already explained to the new recruit that she will be coming to watch you at one or two observation parties. She's has to have training if she is to succeed in the business. Get a commitment from her and then set a time for the training. It helps when you have set times for training sessions. If you can say, "I train on Monday evenings from six thirty until nine o'clock and I look forward to seeing you next Monday at the training," your new recruit knows she needs to be there and she attends. Ah, life is good!

Well, I hate to burst your bubble but it's not always going to be picture perfect. Here's what happens—life.

You are working your direct selling business around your family's schedule and it may be difficult for you to have a set training schedule. If you don't have a set schedule for training you need to have a choice of two different available times when you leave for the interview. You can say, "I've set aside some time for training to help you learn what you need in order to be successful in this business. I can work with you Wednesday from five thirty until eight in the evening, or I can work with you on Saturday morning from nine until noon. Which one's best for you?"

People Who Want to Succeed Will Do What It Takes!

"Sometimes those who need it the most are inclined the least." —Jim Rohn

Those who want to succeed will show up for training, meetings, or anything else beneficial to their success. If they're not attending, they're basically saying to you, "I want to do this business, but I want to do it on my terms." This will happen, but you have to realize not everyone is going to succeed in this business, so don't take it personally. Only twenty percent of the people who join a direct selling business will take it to the level where they can make full-time earnings. The consultants in who are in the twenty percent group all have one key thing in common; they took time to learn the business.

Whether you decide to have one-on-one training, group trainings, or you join a session put on by another leader, try to have training sessions at least every other week. I developed a system of consultant-led group training early in my direct selling career. I discovered that if I taught my leaders how to train, I could have a team of people who were capable of teaching anyone, whether it was their recruit or not, in several different areas. Because we had developed a customized training program for our team, it was much easier to insure every new recruit who came into our organization received the same training. We worked together as a team. We didn't say, "This is my person, so I have to train her." It was more like, "Well, I've got a new recruit this week, but I'm going to be going out of town. I know two other people are going to be having training, so I'll send my new recruit to one of those trainings."

Having a system like this for your team allows for consistent, uniform training and flexibility for the leaders who are teaching. As you grow your leadership team, work with your leaders and encourage them to work with you and the other leaders to create a consistent schedule for training for new recruits.

As I have previously mentioned, new recruits are a lot like children. We can't always assume they're going to do what needs to be done. We'd like to believe our new consultants are going to read their training manuals, but I hate to break it to you—a lot of them don't. As a leader, review the company's consultant guide. This is the number one tool a consultant should refer to. Make sure your new consultants are using the consultant guide. They need to read it, learn from it, and do the things it says to do. As a leader you can help by referring to the consultant guide at your meetings and training sessions.

People are time-challenged. It's becoming more and more difficult to get them to attend meetings. You can have better meeting attendance if you hold them consistently and if you create a meeting schedule at the beginning of each year.

Your monthly meeting is a place to recognize consultants for their accomplishments. To keep your meeting attendance up, make it fun as well as educational. You not only want to train people, you also want to build camaraderie and send them off with plenty of motivation. When your consultants leave the meeting they should feel like the business, their team, and what they've just learned is the best thing ever. *You want them to want to come to the next meeting.*

The more people a leader can involve in her meetings, the more people she'll have at the meetings. I want you to think about this. If you're doing the meeting by yourself and no one else is going to be teaching, you're guaranteed that one person will be there, and that is you. The more people you involve, the more you're likely to have attend.

It's Never Too Early to Have Your First Meeting

I already mentioned that when I first became a leader, I was the "nobody can do anything right but me" type. Because of that, when I look back at my first meetings, I realize they were pretty boring since I was the only one doing any teaching or training. As time went by and I developed other leaders, I started allowing them to teach at the meetings. Once we started having others do different parts to the meeting, it became a lot more fun. It became more about them and it was much easier to increase the attendance.

Now, just so you know, there were only three people at my first meeting: myself and two consultants. It doesn't matter how many people are at your first meeting; it only matters that you begin to have meetings. If you are a new leader your first meeting may very well be in your living room or around your dining room table. As your team grows and you begin to have twenty or more people in attendance, you will most likely want to move to a public location.

There is a very simple outline you can use for your meeting. The first thing you want to do is welcome everyone, especially guests, new recruits, and the leaders you have in attendance. It's always good to let others know how long the leaders have been in the business; then they can see the potential is available for everyone. You can also welcome and introduce people by their levels. You can ask all the guests to stand up, new consultants who have joined in the last thirty days, and leaders of different levels.

There's a lot to recognize in direct selling. If you're a new leader and you're wondering what you want to recognize, think about what you want to have more of. Do you want a higher sales average within your organization, do you want more shows held each month, do you want more recruits? What you recognize you will get more of. You will want to recognize your top salespeople. Your top sellers set an example for the rest of the team. You will also want to recognize the people who are sponsoring and new consultants who complete their "fast start" program, as well as the new leaders in your organization.

This is an example of things to recognize at your monthly meeting:

- New consultants who completed fast start or who held six parties in first thirty days
- Top ten in Personal Sales
- Top rookie (six months or less in the business)
- Highest party for the month
- Most recruits for the month
- Most parties held for the month
- Most qualified recruits for the month
- Company contest winners
- Newly promoted leaders

The educational part of the meeting will be divided into three different parts. You want to have education for increasing sales, getting more bookings, and increasing sponsoring at every meeting. It's best to have a different person teach each of the above topics. If your team is still small it's okay to have someone teach more than one topic, but as your team grows don't forget to involve more people.

You need to review your company's marketing program at every meeting. If you want to create an explosion on your team just watch what happens when every month you begin showing people what they will receive for moving up. There will be a race to see who can become a leader the fastest.

Close your meeting with some type of motivation and maybe a challenge. The desired outcome is to have the attendees pumped up and excited to go home and work their business and come back next month for more of the same!

Who Should You Spend Your Time On?

"A good objective of leadership is to help those who are doing poorly do well and to help those who are doing well to do even better." —Jim Rohn

There are different levels of people a leader will be working with. The first level is her new personally sponsored consultants and recruits who are sponsored by new consultants. These are people who are brand new in the business, and for their first six weeks in the business, the leader should have contact with these new consultants weekly. I suggest coaching or working with your new consultants after every single party for their first six weeks in the business. When you do this you will discover the consultant's strengths and weaknesses within the first few parties. You can help a new consultant who is having problems getting bookings before she has held most of her parties. Think of the advantage she'll have when you talk to her after her first party where she didn't get any bookings. You give her a few suggestions to use for the next party, which she implements, and the following party she gets two new bookings. You are helping her before it's too late.

You're also going to want to talk to and coach your leaders at least once a week. Your leaders are the backbone of your team. The better relationship you have your downline leaders, the more support you'll get from them. Don't think of it as micromanaging, because it is more like updating and motivating.

Then you have consultants on your team who may be one, two, or three levels down from you. You may try calling them once a week for several weeks, and some of them will ignore you. They may not work the business for three-, four-, or five-week stretches at a time. If you've made several attempts to contact someone and you don't hear back from her, the only thing you can do is leave her alone and wait for her to call. Often, the feeling of neglect is enough to make the absentminded consultant pick up the phone to return your call. If she chooses success, then working with her will strengthen her business.

When people on your team don't return your phone calls, it's usually because something's happening in their business. Their business may not be going the way they want it to and they're afraid to let you know. There are a couple things you can do. First of all, any time you call your team members, don't hang up if they don't answer. Leave a friendly message; let them know that you miss them and you're concerned because haven't heard from them in a little while. Let them know you are there for them when they need you.

If you've left a voicemail and still haven't heard from them, send an e-mail message. Make it fun, not threatening. Rather than "I haven't heard from you in a few weeks, so I'm never going to talk to you again" it's more like, "I really miss you. Just wondering how I can help you in the business." If she won't answer her phone, you could also consider a text message. If she ignores that, too, chances are she's trying to get out of the business without hurting your feelings.

When people are a part of your coaching program it's their responsibility to implement the suggestions you give them to help them grow their business. You may have been having weekly contact with someone, but if she's not following through, then you want success for her more than she wants it for herself. You cannot force someone to be successful, and I know how frustrating it can be when we know someone has potential but isn't using it. However, if somebody who has been a part of your coaching program is consistently not returning your calls, drop her. If someone you're continually coaching is not growing or changing her business, stop taking the time from your busy schedule. When she's ready to get back on track, she will call you. The more time you spend working with people who won't change the less time you will have to work with the people who will. The most important thing a leader can do is work with the 20 percent of the people who are producing 80 percent of team volume rather than focusing the majority of your time on the 80 percent of people who are only producing 20 percent of team volume.

Remember, when you're coaching people, you're not a psychologist. It's not your job to listen to their complaints and problems. That's not what coaching is all about. Effective coaching is working with someone who says, "Okay, here's what I did, and these are the results. What can we do to improve the results?" When you are coaching someone you want to find out what she did the previous week, what the results were from the activities that she did, and then offer suggestions as to how she can improve her results.

Coaches Expect Results

"The act of empowering others changes lives, and it's a win-win situation for you and the people you empower." —John Maxwell

A good coach asks more questions. During coaching calls, we often begin to tell people how to do things versus asking them what they did. If you are talking to a new consultant and she says, "I had a three-hundred-dollar party last night, but I didn't get any bookings," you might be tempted to say, "Well, you need to talk about your hostess program more and make sure that you ask every single guest in attendance to book a party."

Instead of telling her what to do, however, you could say, "Well, you had three hundred dollars in sales and eight people showed up to your party, so that's great. Let's find out why you didn't get any bookings. Do you remember what you did to get bookings?" You could ask her simple questions. "How many times did you talk about the hostess program? Did you get a chance to talk to every guest when they were placing their orders? Did you get a chance to talk to every guest about booking a party?" So by asking questions you're getting her to think, *Oh, you know what? I was so nervous I only talked about the hostess program once. I know I'm supposed to talk about the hostess program three times.* So instead of *you* telling her, "Talk about your hostess program three times," you're getting her to figure it out for herself. Then she's going to say, "Okay. From now on I'll remember to talk about it three times." *So the more questions you can ask her, the easier it will be for her to solve her own problems.*

When we provide the questions, they begin to solve their own problems. They begin to provide the solutions instead of us providing the solutions for them. If they provide the solution, they are more likely to implement it.

An important note: make sure you're not trying to coach via e-mail. Coaching should always be done on the phone.

Embracing Technology

Thanks to technology we can now keep in touch with people who live across the country or even on other continents. Teleseminars are a great way to keep in touch with your long-distance team. It's very easy to find a company that will provide you with solutions and a way to train your people at one time on a teleseminar call. You can have weekly teleseminar training, and these calls can be recorded so if someone cannot listen to the live call they can listen to the replay. You can also hold webinars where you could do a live training using a combination of PowerPoint and audio training on the Web. You may have access to online trainings or universities through your company.

If you're providing training through a teleseminar or webinar, you may want to do a roll call so you know who is on the call. You could also have some type of quiz or recognition upon completion of the training. When someone is reluctant to attend trainings it is often a sign they are having problems in the business, and they may need personal contact with the leader.

E-mail is an easy way for leaders to correspond with members of their team, and it's a great way to send out broadcasts or newsletters to your team to keep them informed. It should not be the only means of communication with members of your team, however. Everyone, especially new recruits, needs some personal connection with their sponsor or leader. There are so many different ways to connect with your long-distance team; you shouldn't have any trouble finding a way to keep in touch with everyone.

If you are a leader you should send a newsletter to everyone on your team. I wrote my first newsletter in January 1981 as soon as I became a leader. Even though there were only two other consultants on my team it was fun to recognize one as the Queen and the other one as the Princess. For over twenty-two years I never missed sending a monthly newsletter to my team. Your newsletter is your way of letting members of your team know how important they are to you.

Even if your company has a newsletter that includes recognition, you can also recognize them in your team newsletter. It's another way of seeing their name in print. People get excited about it. In addition to the recognition you want to have content for your newsletter. You can include information about company contests and promotions, new products, and tips to increase sales, bookings, and sponsoring. You can also include a motivation excerpt from a book or magazine. Include a calendar of events for the next several months so everyone has the schedule for trainings, meetings, and teleseminars or webinars. It's also smart to include contest deadlines in the calendar of events just so everything is on one list.

Lead by Example

The number one characteristic of good leaders is a good attitude. No matter what happens, they bounce back. They don't let something or someone get the best of them. They're not a Dr. Jekyll and Mrs. Hyde; if something happens they get over it and move on.

For a leader to be effective she must be an encourager. Just as mothers have to be cheerleaders for their children, leaders need to be supportive of team members. The people on your team will face obstacles and setbacks, and you have to be the person who provides support. You have to be helpful and supportive but still allow them to seek solutions and answers for themselves. It's your obligation to encourage team members while at the same time helping each of them discover their own strengths.

A good leader has to be unwavering. She is focused on the goals she has set for herself and her team. She makes things happen instead of waiting for things to happen. A good leader is confident in her abilities. Newly promoted leaders are often not confident of their abilities to guide; however, the more they learn and grow the more confident they become. That is why it's so important to attend everything you can! The more knowledge you have, the more confident you will become.

Leaders must have integrity. People will follow and support a leader they trust. A successful leader is somebody who supports and does not talk bad about the company. Things happen! You company may choose to make changes that may not be embraced by everyone. A good leader works with members of her team to help them understand the importance of change in every environment.

"Stop expecting those who are different to be what you think they should be. It's never going to happen" —*Wayne Dyer*

It's important to understand that everyone who joins our team is different. People have different agendas for reaching their desired results. People will have various reasons for becoming consultants with your company, and you must recognize and respect people for making their own decisions. As leaders, we are leading a volunteer army, and we need to realize some will not work the business. Some people will not recognize their own potential or will not be willing to work the business in order to succeed. At those times we need to let go. We need to move on and look for more people.

The most rewarding part of my twenty-two years in direct selling was helping other people realize their dreams of becoming a leader and watching how they grew once they became one. My leadership motto was to empower others to be the "best they can be." It's easy to become trapped in the habit of enabling. It is often much easier to tell people what to do, or worse yet to do things for them. The victims of enabling continually struggle to be self-sufficient, so I again encourage you to "empower others" by holding them accountable to pursue their own dreams and goals. Teach your leaders the skills that will give them the confidence to pursue their dreams and goals.

My definition of a good leader is *"someone who brings out the best in others."* It is the special person who discovers the nugget of potential in each individual—whether it be a great personality, a hunger for knowledge, or good organizational or people skills—and brings it to the surface so they will flourish. Legendary Leadership™ means helping people achieve things they never believed they were capable of. Your recognition as a leader comes from the successes of your leaders and consultants. The more you help others the more you'll enjoy being a leader with your company!

"For most, careers unfold slowly and over time. Every stage is a proving ground. Only after we have mastered each stage are we given the opportunity to move forward. It takes time at each stage to build a foundation for future success, to learn the lessons we must learn and develop the skills we will need for the future." —Chris Widener

Leader Tip: Encourage newly promoted leaders to begin sending a team newsletter their first month.

Leader Tip: Encourage newly promoted leaders to hold a small get-together periodically with their team.

Leader Tip: Don't smother your team!

Are you afraid you won't

be able to balance it all?

Read on…

CHAPTER NINE

How to Maintain a "Lifestyle Friendly" Business

"Believing life is a positive, fun-filled experience produces that reality." —Wally Amos

The most important thing you can do to create and maintain more balance in your personal and business life is to create consistency in your schedule. The less stops and starts you have with your direct selling business, the easier it will be to make sure your business is blending and meshing with everything you have going on in your personal life. You may have a period of inactivity for one or two weeks and then overcompensate by scheduling three or four parties the following week. All of a sudden, it becomes interruptive to your household and to your family. Now you are gone for four nights in a row instead of the normal two nights per week you normally go out. The more consistency you develop, the less stops and starts you have and the easier it will be to keep the balance between your personal and your business life.

You need to think about the reality. Do you find yourself complaining you are spending too much time on your business? When somebody says that, my first question is, "How are you spending your time? How many parties did you do last week or month?" She may have done four parties last month, at an average of three hours per party, which is only twelve hours she was actually out working her business. If somebody tells me the business is consuming all her time, then I need to know exactly what she is spending time on. Maybe she's not getting bookings dated in while she's at the party and is spending all her time chasing down leads on the phone. Maybe she's spending a lot of time on the Internet.

There are a lot of things that can absorb time, but not all of them will produce income. Checking e-mails and being on the Internet all day long are time wasters. How many times do you check your e-mails each day? How many times do you get in chat rooms? People can often become very busy and still get very little done.

When someone claims the business is taking all their time and they do not have the sales or recruits to support this claim, a red flag goes up. The individual needs to discover why she is not working the business as efficiently as she can be.

Create a Family Support System

"One person caring about another represents life's greatest value." —Jim Rohn

I was very lucky to have a supportive husband in the business. Larry never held me back from pursuing my goals and dreams with the business. He and my two sons were always supportive of me and my desire to grow my business. The easiest way for a consultant to get her family's support in the business is to engage them in helping with small tasks and allowing them to see and enjoy some of the rewards.

For example, let's say when you joined your company your goal was to earn some money to take your family on a vacation. You work your business for six months and your family is no closer to taking a vacation than they were six months ago. They will become discouraged and begin to question your judgment. In the same situation, if you had taken time to establish a new savings account and had built it up by a few thousand dollars, they would understand that although it might take a little longer at least the family is closer to going on vacation. You could even have a chat with everyone to let them know how close you are and what you still need to do. You could take them shopping for something they will need for the trip. In doing this, you keep the family engaged with your pursuit of the goal and supportive of your business.

I'll admit I was not above bribing my kids with toys or baseball cards in exchange for a few hours of getting my catalogs, order forms, and other supplies ready for me. One of the wonderful things my direct selling business provided was many happy vacations that we would not have had the additional money for had I not been working. It was encouraging to look around our house and see televisions, stereos, computers, copiers, and many other extras I earned in company contests that we could enjoy as a family. The more you can show the results of your efforts, the happier and more supportive your family will be. Oh, the diamonds and jewels were a perk for me, too!

Of course, the little extras are one of the reasons some people join. You may be working the business for income to provide some of the extras you don't have enough money for at the end of each month. Spread the wealth. If your husband isn't supportive of your business but has a hobby or interest like golf, take some of your earnings and buy him a new set of clubs or a round at a top course. I guarantee he will become a believer because you thought to include him in the rewards of your business. Don't worry, if you make sure you're consistent with your schedule there will be plenty of money left over to shop for shoes!

The more you bring yourself back to why you began your business, the easier it will become for you to create a business that works for you. You are a business owner. Whether you have a direct selling business or a brick-and-mortar storefront, you need to plan ahead for the ups and downs. Planning ahead will prevent you from throwing in the towel when things aren't going as well as you would like. You need to revisit and understand the reasons you began your direct selling business and why it is important for you to keep it going. My desire to be home with my sons and not have to leave the kids in daycare kept me focused on the business. You need to know what it is that will get you through any tough times.

Passion Helps You Maintain Focus

The easiest way for you to keep your passion for the business is to keep working. The more you work your business, the easier you will find it is to keep the passion and spark alive. Having a gratitude list of things you are grateful for in your business will help maintain the desire to keep focused and working. Once you win a contest prize or a trip, and you realize you never would have had the chance otherwise, you'll notice a change in your attitude and in your business.

Having your own direct selling business is a lot like marriage. When you begin dating and then become newlyweds there's a lot of passion and sparks are flying. Then after a few years you develop a routine; the more habitual it becomes, the easier it is to lose that passion. You need to go back and say, "Okay, why did I fall in love with this person in the first place? How do I bring the passion back?"

Your business is no different from anything else in your life. If it's worth having, it's worth working for. Frequently, the more we work our business, the more we begin to take it for granted. The more we take things for granted, the easier it is to have lower results. You have to go back and reexamine what needs to be done to keep that spark alive, just as you would in your marriage.

You will maintain your focus in your business when you set your goals and write them down.

- What do you want to accomplish?
- When do you want to accomplish it by?
- Why do you want to accomplish it?
- What will happen as a result of you reaching this goal?
- Who will you become as a result of reaching this goal?

Then create your action plan.

119

- What are the steps that I need to take in order to reach this goal?
- What do I need to do each day to put me closer to my goal?
- What do I need to do this week to put me closer to my goal?
- What do I need to do this month to put me closer to my goal?

Let's say, for instance, you want to become a leader with your company and you need to sponsor five people to reach the first leadership level. You have set a target date by saying, "I want to become a leader within the next three months." You need to sponsor two people a month. Now you need to create an action plan to sponsor two people each month. You need to ask yourself, "What am I going to do to in order to get these two people each month?" Your plan could be as simple as, "Each and every month I will hold a minimum of eight parties. From each of these parties I will find at least three people to send information home with, which will provide me with twenty-four leads from my parties each month. I will interview at least two people each week. From these eight interviews, I will easily sponsor at least two people."

Set a Goal, Write It Down, Break It Down into Steps, Create an Action Plan

As soon as you reach a personal or business goal, it's very important for you to set a new goal. One of the biggest obstacles in this industry is that we reach to a certain level, and then sit back, bask in the glory, and never move forward again. You may breathe a sigh of relief, and then you forget to do the same activities that got you where you are. You may even begin to slide backwards.

The same is true when you reach a personal goal. You may work really hard to set aside four thousand dollars for your family vacation, and then all of a sudden once you return home you have nothing new to motivate you. Once you have accomplished a goal, whether it's a personal or business goal, you always need to think to ask yourself this question: "What's next?"

It's great when your company offers incentives, promotions, or contests for trips or prizes. The danger comes when you develop the habit of only working when your company has an incentive. If you are only incentive-driven your company may announce a new contest and when you review the prize brochure you may think to yourself, *Oh, there's nothing I really want.* When this happens, you sit back and don't work as hard as you would have had you been trying to earn a prize. When you aren't working your business consistently you will notice a decrease in your bookings, activity, and income. Your lack of motivation spills over to every aspect of your business. It's easy to see how short-term inactivity can cause long-term damage to your business.

Make sure you set an earnings goal for your business. If you do this, you'll most likely discover if you reach your earnings goal you will have more than enough to earn your company's incentives. If you find yourself a little short for a contest, increase your monetary goal to coincide with the current contest. When you do this you will also find your business becoming more consistent.

I must admit that in addition to the incredible income I realized in direct selling, I loved earning a free trip every year. I really feel one of the reasons I spent over twenty-two years in direct selling is because I won an incentive trip the first full year in my business! I earned my first trip in 1981 and Larry and I went to Maui, Hawaii, in May of 1982. I wonder what would have happened and where I would be today if I had not won that first trip. You are vacationing with top sellers, home office staff, and the owner of your company. You go on one trip, and when you return home you are more excited. Once you taste success, once you win an incentive trip, you're hooked! There is no going back! There is no way you won't earn next year's incentive trip.

Once I went to Hawaii in 1982, I never missed a company incentive trip. It is definitely a wonderful way to have a fantastic vacation by yourself, with your husband/significant other, and occasionally when allowed with your children. You should definitely work on your company's incentive trips. They are certainly part of what makes this a lifestyle-friendly business.

Create an Effective Home Office

Another reason this is a lifestyle-friendly business is that you can work from home, which is great news. The bad news is, because people know you work from home, they think you're open for business twenty-four hours a day, seven days a week. There were a few steps I needed to take early in my career in order to achieve balance between my business and personal life.

One of the first things I did was to have a separate phone for my business, and I kept my personal line unlisted. Having a line that was used exclusively for business allowed me the flexibility to set business hours. My answering machine was on when I was not available and my business hours were stated on the answering machine. If you decide to heed this advice your message could be simply, "Hi, this is Karen. Thank you for calling me. My office is open from nine a.m. until four p.m. Monday through Friday. Please leave your name, phone number, and a brief message and I will return your call as soon as possible during my working hours."

A recorded message like this will advise people who are calling that you are not available twenty-four/seven. There's no emergency that cannot wait until your office is open. Is it life-threatening if someone received the wrong products? Is it worth disrupting your family's schedule over? Most likely any call you receive can wait until nine o'clock tomorrow morning.

The second thing you can do to keep your business lifestyle-friendly is to identify when you are available to work your business. By taking time to set boundaries in the beginning you will set an example for others who may want to join you in the business. You will be demonstrating to people exactly what you are telling them. "Hey, you know what? The great news is that you can run your business from your home and work the hours you choose to work." Once you begin to take control of your business and your hours, and decide not to let your business control you, you will be more pleased with your business. You won't become frustrated and disenchanted with running a business from your home.

You need to have time for yourself and time for your family. My husband and I had date nights every Friday night. When the boys were young they sometimes came along, but most of the time we hired a sitter and had a few hours to ourselves. Of course I scheduled lots of family time, too. Baseball, basketball, football, and hockey games occupied a good deal of my time, and I made it a priority to attend. Planning family time kept me from focusing on business twenty-four hours a day, seven days a week, which is easy to do when your office is where you live. Sticking to your business hours and being available for your family helps them understand they are just as important as your business is!

There will be times when somebody joins a direct selling company and realizes that it's more time consuming than she believed it would be. Maybe she's working a full-time job and underestimated how much time a well-run home business would take. She has to ask herself, "Why did I join this? What was I hoping to accomplish from this direct selling business? Is this still what I want to accomplish? How can I find the time to make it work?"

Why doesn't she have the time to work her business? Is there something happening in her life that's taking a lot of time away from the business? Is it a family issue? Is it her full-time job? Is it because she is not organized and doesn't have the time to get things done? If this has happened or is happening to you, it's time to ask yourself some questions to get to the root of what is preventing you from being in balance. It may be a time management issue you can solve by becoming better organized. Once you begin asking yourself questions you'll probably realize you *do* have time to work your business. You just need to be a little bit more structured. Once you discipline yourself to focus on working your business around your schedule and doing activities that produce income, you'll find out it doesn't take a lot of time.

You will even find that once you become disciplined you can even take a break from your business if you need to and start it up again. I won't say it's not without its challenges, because the more continuity you have in your business, the easier your business becomes. It's great to know your business will be there when you get back. If you have to take a break from your business, say for maternity leave or to take care of a parent who is ill; try to prepare for it in advance. When you are holding parties the last month before you're getting ready for your maternity leave, for example, begin to prepare for your business to be there when you return. You can say, "As you can see, the good news is I'm going to be having a baby soon. The bad news is I'm not going to be able to do your home party until after this bundle of joy arrives." Begin to book dates for when you plan to return to your business. Go ahead and prepare for their booking, get their guest list back, and have everything ready exactly as if they were booking a party two weeks from now. Even if the party is six or seven weeks out instead of two, you'll still be ready to go. Once you have the baby and are ready to restart your business, you've got everything in place. You'll mail the invitations and hit the ground running as soon as you come back from your leave.

Having your own direct selling business should add to your pleasure and allow you to have some of the things you might not have otherwise. It's fun, challenging, rewarding, and one of the greatest ways I know of to add considerable income in the least amount of time. Take time to enjoy your business, and your business can help you enjoy your life!

"Learn how to be happy with what you have while you pursue all that you want." —Jim Rohn

How do you

make it last?

Read on...

CHAPTER TEN

Discover the Secrets to Success and Longevity in Direct Selling

*"There are two ways to live your life.
One is as though nothing is a miracle.
The other is as though everything is
a miracle." —Albert Einstein*

When I first joined direct selling, it was to make an extra hundred dollars a week, so never in my wildest dreams did I even contemplate this business spanning twenty-plus years. As I look back I realized most of what happened over the years was good. I was experiencing great results and having the time of my life! I was so satisfied with my earnings and our family's lifestyle, and so fulfilled by my accomplishments, that there were no obstacles I couldn't overcome.

There were plenty of times over the years, however when I wanted to throw in the towel and just say, "Forget it. It is definitely not worth it." What did I do to maintain focus? Well, I remembered seeing my son standing there in the daycare window, crying and reaching for me as I left for work. It was then I knew a traditional job wasn't an option for me; I couldn't turn back. I had to keep setting my goals, and I had to keep working the business no matter what happened. Whatever obstacle came my way, I'd say, "Is this obstacle bigger than me, or am I bigger than this obstacle?" I just never gave up! I didn't give up on myself and my desire to be home with my sons, and I didn't give up on my dream of being successful in direct selling.

I don't have any regrets. I think everything happens for a reason. I know it was the right time for me to make this business work. A few years ago when I was talking to my sons, who are now grown, I asked, "What do you think about me being in this business?" They said, "Mom, the one thing we know is you were there for us whenever we needed you. We remember you being at all of our activities and big events." I don't know if I would have had the opportunity to have such an active part of everything they did if I hadn't had my own direct selling business. They remember the prizes and rewards and the trips we took them on. We took both of our kids to Hawaii three times and we took them on wonderful trips to Disney World and other US destinations. I know I wouldn't have had the ability to do those things had it not been for my direct selling business. I look at what my business provided me over the years and I can definitely say I have no regrets. There is absolutely nothing I would have changed.

The first thing you can do to create more success in your business is to realize, first of all, that this is a people business. Believe it or not, you are helping people when you introduce them to your product. Your company has wonderful products, and by presenting someone with the opportunity to host a party you are helping them earn items they like at a substantial savings. The nature of the business is to help people who are struggling to make ends meet. You are helping them in more ways than by just providing products. You are changing their life.

Three Life-Changing Questions

"Be what you are, and become what you are capable of becoming." Robert Louis Stevenson

There are three questions everyone needs to ask themselves. The first one is, "Am I going where I want to go and is my life moving in the direction I want?" The second one is, "Am I doing what I want to do?" And the third question everybody needs to ask themselves is, "Am I being who I want to be?" These questions help you discover your purpose in life. When you discover your purpose you will be well on your way to living happily ever after.

The most important thing you can do to begin creating a more successful direct selling business is to challenge yourself. Do this by increasing your goals. Challenge yourself to become a little bit better, whether it's a monthly challenge or a yearly challenge. Maybe you sold forty thousand dollars last year; this year set a goal for fifty thousand. If you are competitive by nature, you may want to have "friendly competition" with other people. I always wanted to be number one, and

I held several number one positions with my direct selling companies over the years. I challenged Marlene Cain, one of the leaders, and we had a friendly competition throughout the year. Just for the record my team ended up number one for the second six months of the year and number two for the year but we still did over a half-million more than we had done the previous year!

In order for you to be successful in your direct selling business you need to quit looking for excuses. Quit looking for excuses why the business is not working or why certain things aren't happening, and begin to look for answers instead. You can either look for excuses or you can look for solutions, and I guarantee if you look for excuses you will continually find more. If you begin to look for solutions, you'll find everything you need to succeed. Hopefully, you've found some of them in the pages of this book.

What I Wish I Had Known Sooner

People have asked what I know now that I wish I knew when I was getting started. Well, what I really needed to know was the importance of sponsoring right away and how to get my first recruit in the business. I went several months in my direct selling business before I brought my first person in because I was like the typical direct seller: I wanted to wait. I wasn't sure I knew enough to sponsor right away, so I never asked anyone. I was sponsored by my mom who was an awesome trainer. I also had great teachers and mentors in the business, but I wish they had prodded me a little bit more in my early months. Even though my business was okay, I believe it could have been better in the beginning. I wish I had been held a little bit more accountable by people to do more. It could be one of the reasons I worked so hard with my new recruits. After my challenging start and my inability to sponsor, I realized how important it is to create good habits immediately.

What you need to do now is decide. Decide what you want from your direct selling business. You could be in the early stages of your direct selling career and thinking, *Okay. You know what? I am reading this book and I'm realizing that I can achieve anything that I want to accomplish.* You need to know what you want, how much you want to earn, and what you're willing to do in order to reach your goals.

If you're in the stage of your business where you're in a little slump, ask yourself, "What do I want to accomplish?" You picked up this book because you wanted to build a better business. If there's something in the contents you've discovered you're not doing but should be, then hopefully I've helped you get over that hump and you'll now move forward to success.

This is time to determine what you want to do and how you are going to get it done. What steps are you going to take? What changes are you going to make? What are you going to do right now to get the results you want from your direct selling business?

If you liked what you read in this book and you want to know a little bit more, visit my website, www.karenphelps.com, where you can find several direct selling training and motivational programs. If you are interested in teleseminar trainings, past articles, and group coaching, go to www.directsellingdoctor.com to find out how to make the most of your direct selling business.

If you take nothing else away from this book, know this: if you put people first, you will succeed. You won't have to think twice about it. Your business will happen for you. It comes back to the Golden Rule, "Do unto others as you want others to do unto you." The better you treat people, the better you treat yourself and your business, the more you will be rewarded.

I believe in you! You are an incredible person who can have anything you want! It's time to stake your claim and pursue your dreams! YOU ARE AWESOME!

What's your next Step?

Check out the motivational and direct selling resources available at www.karenphelps.com

Books:

It's a Party Out There© – Keeping the Fun and Profit in Direct Selling

DVDs:

It's a Party Out There© - Keeping the Fun and Profit in Direct Selling

CDs:

It's a Party Out There© - Keeping the Fun and Profit in Direct Selling
Build Your Bookings
Increase Your Party Attendance
Overcoming Objections
Hostess Coaching
Goal Getting
Spontaneous Sponsoring
Presentation Pizzazz
Excelling in Direct Selling
Time Management
Overcoming Your Sponsoring Phobia
Put Your Big Girl Panties On and Deal With It
Change Your Mindset to Change Your Reality
Master the Mechanics of Mentoring

For personal coaching contact our office: support@karenphelps.com

For teleseminar training contact our office: Karen@karenphelps.com

To hire Karen to speak to your company or team email:
Karen@karenphelps.com or call our Office (248) 625-4897

IF YOU DON'T KNOW HOW TO TAKE YOUR DIRECT SELLING BUSINESS TO THE NEXT LEVEL YOU NEED TO LEARN FROM SOMEONE WHO WILL SHOW YOU HOW!

There's only one way left for you to earn the income you deserve...

Surround yourself with others who have similar goals and the mindset that "If You Believe, You Can Achieve."

YOUR MEMBERSHIP IN DIRECT SELLING DOCTOR WILL HELP...

Motivate ... you to pursue your goals

Stimulate... ideas you can use to catapult to greatness

Excite... so that you look forward to each and every day

Inspire... if these folks can succeed, so can I

Unlock... your potential

Eliminate... obstacles that stand between you and your goals

Overcome... adversity to live your dreams

Discover... the habits and techniques of modern achievers in Direct Selling

THIS PROGRAM IS FOR YOU IF ...

You are ready to be a top-notch WORKING DIRECT SELLER

You have the burning desire to DOUBLE or TRIPLE your income this year

You want to be making upwards of $50K CONSISTENTLY

You're self-motivated, resourceful, reliable, and a quick study

You're ready to DO WHATEVER IT TAKES to kick your business into high gear!!!

These are just a few of the benefits you'll enjoy as a "Direct Selling Doctor Inner Circle member"...

- Weekly Audio or Video Tips sent directly to your email ($25 value)
- Monthly Articles from myself and other success experts ($50 value)
- Access to Karen's archive of articles (Priceless)
- Access to Karen's Million Dollar success experts through monthly "Interview Teleseminars" - Listen in as Karen interviews experts of all kinds during a "member only teleseminar" (MP3 available after call- $100 value)
- Our Treasure Chest of Recommended Resources. (We've spent hours compiling some of the finest sources for additional tips, tricks, and motivation - into just one location so that you'll have immediate access when you need them. And we've personally checked each one of them out ... separating the good, quality resources from the tons of bad ones... so you won't waste your valuable time. Think of our Treasure Chest as your golden rolodex of references you can use in achieving success in your personal and professional lives. (Priceless!)
- A special shopping cart to purchase most of Karen's products at a discounted price (Priceless)

AS A GOLD + TELE-COACHING MEMBER YOU WILL RECEIVE ALL OF THE ITEMS LISTED ABOVE PLUS... THE FOCUS OF THE "GOLD + TELE-COACHING" WILL BE LEARNING HOW TO COACH AND MENTOR YOUR TEAM.

- Monthly special "closed door", Group Coaching Call (10 members will be selected each month to ask Karen a question about their business. The questions must not be company specific. These 10 people will be given a separate access code to allow them to participate while the other attendees listen in) MP3 of call will be posted on the website. ($100 value)
- At least one random member each month will be selected to receive a one hour coaching call ($300 Value)
- All members will be able to listen to the live coaching call or download the MP3 file ($100 value)
- Free CD of Monthly Teleseminar Call ($50 value)

- GOLD + "ONLY" FREE NETWORKING EVENT at Yearly Seminar which will be held in 2009 ($150 value)
- Up to a 50% off registration for all Karen Phelps Sponsored Seminars (Priceless!)
- Gold + Restricted Access Website (Priceless!)
- Member Recognition on Website (we'll be recognizing some of our members achievements as they implement ideas and grow their businesses) (Priceless)
- Special Members Only Shopping Cart with discount prices on most of Karen Phelps' products. (Priceless)

Bonus #1 - Free E-Book *Inspirational Leadership- How to Become a Motivating Leader* (Karen Phelps interviews Stan Toler $45 Value)

Bonus #2 - Free E- Book *Creating Consistency* ($45 Value)

Bonus #3 - Mp3 Download - "Inspirational Leadership" Interview with Stan Toler ($45 value)

Bonus #4 - MP3 Download - "Ask Karen Phelps Part 1" ($45 Value)

Bonus $5 - MP3 Download - "Ask Karen Phelps Part 2" ($45 Value)

Go to www.directsellingdoctor.com for more information.